MAKE Your Life PRIME TIME

MAKE Your Life PRIME TIME

How to Have It All Without Losing Your Soul

María Celeste Arrarás

ATRIA BOOKS

NEW YORK LONDON TORONTO SYDNEY

ATRIA BOOKS
A Division of Simon & Schuster, Inc.
1230 Avenue of the Americas
New York, NY 10020

First Atria Books hardcover edition May 2009

ATRIA BOOKS and colophon are trademarks of Simon & Schuster, Inc.

For information about special discounts for bulk purchases, please contact Simon & Schuster Special Sales at 1-866-506-1949 or business@simonandschuster.com.

The Simon & Schuster Speakers Bureau can bring authors to your live event. For more information or to book an event contact the Simon & Schuster Speakers Bureau at 1-866-248-3049 or visit our website at www.simonspeakers.com.

Manufactured in the United States of America

1 3 5 7 9 10 8 6 4 2

Library of Congress Cataloging-in-Publication Data
Arrarás, María Celeste.
Make your life prime time : How to have it all without losing your soul / María Celeste Arrarás.
p. cm.
1. Arrarás, María Celeste. 2. Television journalists—Puerto Rico—Biography. I. Title.
PN4946.A77 A3 2009
070.92 B 22 2008034431

ISBN-13: 978-1-4165-8582-4

In homage to Astrid Mangual and José Enrique Arrarás, my parents, who gave me life and helped shape my character. I hope that after reading this book, my children are as grateful to and proud of me as I am of their grandparents.

CONTENTS

PROLOGUE

I always knew there would come a time when I finally would put on paper the book I'd been writing in my mind for years.

That moment came one night in 2007, when I arrived home from work later than usual and discovered three lumps under my bedsheets. My children—Julian, Adrian, and Lara—had fallen asleep in my bed, waiting for me to come home. There was less room for me in the bed that night, but I didn't care. I squeezed in next to them, feeling guilty about not being there earlier to spend time with them, and yearning for that feeling of well-being that comes when I can pull them close.

They were sound asleep, and when I lowered the bedsheet to kiss them good night, I got the scare of my life: Those were not my kids!

Instead of my "babies," I found three enormous children taking up practically the whole bed. No wonder there was hardly any room for me.

After a few moments that seemed like an eternity, I realized that my children had neither been kidnapped, nor was I hallucinating. My little ones had suddenly grown up, in the blink of an eye, and I had not fully realized it until that moment. I suddenly felt the sensation that life was passing me by at lightning speed. A thousand mixed emotions rushed through me, but the main one was fear—fear that I would blink again and they would be all grown up. That I would die without having taught them so many things. Fear of the inevitable—that one day soon, each one would go out into the world alone, without me by their side protecting them unconditionally.

At that moment, I knew it was time to open their eyes.

That night, I could not close my own. Sitting on the corner of the bed, I began writing this book that I hope my children will use as a compass to safely navigate the turbulent sea of life.

It's a guide of life lessons I have learned over the years, and I hope it will offer them direction in tough times. This is my legacy . . . my very essence. The book I wish I had read when I was growing up. May it serve as a shield that protects them from danger and from themselves.

I owe it to myself and to them—before their next metamorphosis.

MAKE
Your Life
PRIME TIME

1

LOVE SHOULDN'T BE THE SOLE MASTER OF YOUR DESTINY.

Yes, it is possible to learn from someone else's mistakes.

My mother is a remarkable woman who speaks three languages, plays the piano like a concert pianist, has a degree in chemistry, and can talk about almost anything. Yet when it came to matters of the heart, she admits that she sacrificed her dreams and aspirations for love. Over and over again.

One thing she did right was to make sure that I didn't do the same. And I never have.

She married my father two months after graduating magna cum laude with a chemistry degree. Although she had been awarded a scholarship to continue her studies in Belgium, she heeded her mother's advice and followed my father to England, where he, too, had been awarded a scholarship. After all, back then, when a woman got married, she was expected to stay home and raise the children.

And that's what she did. As a wife, she was the perfect complement to my father, who eventually became the chancellor of the University of Puerto Rico in Mayagüez, where my sister and I were born. After classes, she gathered several professors at our house on campus and they would spend long hours discussing philosophy, literature, and the arts. We had a good life and enjoyed the perks that came with my father's position—a chef, a chauffeur, and a live-in nanny.

But my parents' divorce changed all that. My father left the university to pursue a political career, and my mother, my sister, and I moved into my grandmother's apartment in San Juan. It was a tough time. My father was running for mayor of San Juan and, not having an income, he was struggling to pay our private school tuition and to send my mother her $500 monthly alimony. My mother had no choice but to look for a job. It was a rude awakening. She had to compete with younger professionals with master's degrees and doctorates. And after being out of her field for more than a decade, most of what she had learned had become obsolete in the face of technological advances.

She was a housewife with no house and no husband.

I saw her go from a life of privilege as the spouse of the university chancellor to a life of uncertainty working entry-level jobs to make ends meet. She struggled unbelievably, both financially and in rediscovering who she was as a person.

And in the process, she made sure that we learned by example. She would always tell me, "Brains over beauty, Mari. Studying hard and having a career is the only insurance in life."

At thirteen, I started to take on babysitting jobs so I could afford the nice outfits all teenagers fancy. I will always remember the day I walked into a Lerner's with my hard-earned twenty dollars and bought myself a red shirt with white letters that read "peace and love." It was my prized possession.

My mother got a job working for the University of Puerto Rico at an agricultural experimental station, where she met the man who would become her second husband—a Peruvian doctor who soon received a residency opportunity in New Jersey.

Then she did it again. She sacrificed her profession for love, chose to follow him, and together they eventually had two sons. My sister and I were in the middle of the school year, so it was decided that we would stay with my father and his new wife.

In New Jersey, my mother stayed at home with their sons, one of whom developed severe mental retardation and autism as a result of an undiagnosed thyroid deficiency. Unable to deal with a handicapped child, her husband left her after eight years of marriage. A few months later he stopped paying child support.

I remember her telling me, "Never put your life in the hands of a man. Make sure you are always self-sufficient, economically independent, so that you don't have to go through what I'm going through."

But nothing she told me has shaped me more than watching the woman I respect most in the world pick up the pieces of her life and start anew—a second time.

She was at a bigger disadvantage—older, in a different city, and all alone. But she pulled through. Thanks to her academic background and language skills, she eventually got an entry-level job at an international pharmaceutical company and worked her way up to middle management.

She worked about forty miles from home, so she would get up at four in the morning to make breakfast for the family, shower, and rush out of the house. There was no time to dry her hair, so in the winter, icicles formed by the time she reached her car. A few times after a long day of hard work she fell asleep at the wheel. Thankfully, she never had an accident. My mother always says that an angel was with her, because angels protect mothers who are left alone to care for their children. She believes that if mothers do the best they can, God will handle the rest.

She spent sixteen years working hard and raising my brothers. The oldest graduated from college with honors and, at my mother's insistence, continued on to complete his master's degree.

Although my mother never achieved her full potential professionally, her sacrifice was rewarded when she met a fellow scientist who had never been married and had no children. They became husband and wife shortly thereafter, and he has been a real father to my handicapped brother.

As a result of my mother's experience, I vowed that I was going to get an education, and I was going to have a career. And I was never going to leave my destiny in the hands of a man. That's not to say I didn't want to fall in love, or be married, or have children. I simply wanted to be the owner of my own decisions. I didn't want to be in a situation where I lost at love and lost at life as a consequence.

I went to Loyola University in New Orleans on financial aid and worked odd jobs to make extra cash and pay six hundred dollars for my first car. I scooped ice cream all day at Häagen-Dazs, and at night had to take aspirin to relieve the pain in my wrists. At another job, at a health food restaurant, I had to don a moon suit whenever I took the chocolate-dipped bananas into the freezer. I worked as a waitress, serving hamburgers and pizza for meager tips, and mopped the floors at closing time. And I put up with some really nasty customers.

I graduated from college with a communications degree, and so did my boyfriend at the time. But instead of me following him, he followed me. He moved to Puerto Rico, even though he didn't speak Spanish. The relationship didn't last long after that.

A couple of years after marrying my first husband, I was offered the opportunity of a lifetime: to enter the Hispanic television market as the anchor of an important station in New York City. And driven by his selfless love, my husband let me go. But living in different cities, we grew apart and eventually divorced.

My career took me from San Juan to New York to Los Angeles to Miami. I felt like a gypsy. In five years, I lived in four different cities. And even though I managed to fall deeply in love, I moved every time my job required it. My love was strong, but the fear of ending up like my mother was stronger.

I met my second husband after living in Miami for several years. At that point I was ready to settle down and have a home. We had many happy times and three beautiful children. But trying to juggle family and a successful career took all my energy. I was so determined to be the perfect wife, mother, and professional that I never saw it coming: He started seeing someone else.

The night I found out, I couldn't close my eyes. Yet the next morning, anxious and exhausted as I was, I was on a flight to New York for a scheduled meeting with the president of NBC. It took everything I had to stay focused during that meeting, which was so important to my career. Again, I wasn't going to let anything interfere with my goals, my independence, not even one of the most painful disappointments of my life.

I have learned that it is possible to find love—true, passionate, meaningful love—more than once. But there's a difference between giving your love to someone and letting yourself get lost in love.

I know that if I had not learned that distinction, my second divorce would have not only devastated me emotionally but also ruined me financially. For nearly ten years, I was enriched by that relationship, but I wasn't defined by it. I had established myself and my career independent of my ex-husband. Before that relationship and since, I continue to have my own identity. The only person who should define you in life is you.

That doesn't mean it's easy. Not long ago, I was days away from embarking on a trip to Africa with someone I cared for tremendously when I received a call from the *Today* show. Once again, they wanted me to cohost the program. Unfortunately it was on the same day we were supposed to depart. That meant having to rearrange several connecting flights, which could potentially derail our entire trip. My boyfriend didn't take the news well, and for the first time in my life, I wondered if I should follow my heart.

When I called my agent and friend Raúl Mateu to share my predicament, he didn't hesitate:

"Any guy who wants you to give up a great opportunity like this one isn't worth it," he told me. "Take it from the other man in your life. When you do the *Today* show, all the guys in the United States are going to fall all over you!"

Ultimately, my boyfriend understood. He was that kind of guy. And not only did I do the show, but we went to Africa the next day.

Some people may judge me as calculating or unromantic. But nothing is further from the truth. To give yourself in a relationship, you need to be whole; otherwise you have nothing to offer. And that can be accomplished only by achieving your goals as an individual. Then, and only then, will you be able to choose a partner based on his or her human qualities and not on your insecurities or financial needs. And when you give your heart, that person will know it was earned for all the right reasons.

2

BE THE BEST OF THE BEST OR THE WORST OF THE WORST. NEVER MEDIOCRE.

The rest of the house was quiet, still shrouded in night, when my father would wake me up at five a.m. to swim.

I was a slow starter in the mornings. Like any eight-year-old, I occasionally let sleep drag me back down to the bed, but the thought of my father coming in and finding me out was enough to unglue me from the sheets. My father helped put me in the right frame of mind for this daily chore. By the time

I was dressed, with my swimsuit under my school uniform, he had already cooked breakfast and had my ten wheat germ energy pills set out for me on the kitchen counter. Yes, it was brutally early. But it was also a special time for my father and me, because during this time I had him all to myself. Like most brilliant people, my father either had a short attention span or he hyperfocused; when I swam he was completely present and focused only on me.

At that early hour, the other members of my swim team were probably still in bed. I thought about them, warm in their sheets, as we drove to the Olympic-sized pool on the campus of the University of Puerto Rico–Mayagüez. They were hours away from waking up for school. Whenever sleepiness intoxicated me enough to let me voice any of those thoughts, my father set me straight: If I wanted to be an average swimmer with average success, then I should just skip these morning workouts and the ones we had on the weekends and simply stick to the regular after-school swimming schedule practices with the team's coach.

Once facing the pool, I dreaded going into the cold water. But to my father, there was no use wasting time pondering the issue.

"Don't stick your toe in the pool, Mari," he would

tell me. "If you think it's too cold, you'll never jump in."

Even though I was so young, I knew he was right. So I would take a deep breath and count down. *Five . . . four . . . three . . . two . . . one . . . splash!*

"Hesitation is for the average and I'm not raising you to be average," my father would say. It reminded me of the time I brought home a C on my report card. He looked at it silently for a couple of minutes and then sat me down for a brief but lasting lesson.

"Bring me an A or an F. Never a C. You should be the best of the best or the worst of the worst. But never mediocre."

I knew he was serious. He had endless duties as chancellor of the university, and the fact that he made time to be my personal coach was not lost on me. Whenever I won a competition, whenever I beat my own time, his eyes would twinkle with pride, making me feel that the sacrifice was worth it.

You have to understand something about my father: When he wants something, he really goes for it. Once, he decided he wanted to own chow chows. So he bought the encyclopedia of chow chows and figured out which dogs were bred from the most famous lineage. The dog on the cover would be the grandfather of the dog we owned. When he got into fish, he ended up having ten 55-gallon and four 110-gallon aquariums; he had to build an entire room just for his fish. Later, he started a collection of pre-Columbian art and ended up amassing the largest private collection in all of Latin America. He has degrees in political science, economics, and law from Ivy League universities in the United States and Europe. When he took the bar, he achieved the highest score ever recorded in the Caribbean. My father lives and breathes excellence.

No one challenged my father to do better and better, to keep improving and learning and striving. His motivation has always come from within. He didn't settle for being the chancellor of the University of Puerto Rico–Mayagüez. He challenged himself and ran for mayor of San Juan, became secretary of housing, the president of the island's Olympic committee, and eventually one of the most influential legislators ever in Puerto Rico. Whatever he does, he does to the exquisite extreme. And it was just so when it came to my swimming.

He never stopped feeding me information. He bought videos of Olympic champions filmed with underwater cameras showing off their swimming techniques, and we studied them together. He was on top of all the latest trends, and thanks to his vision, our team was one of the first in Latin

America to exchange nylon swimsuits for ultra-light Lycra ones that absorbed less water and had less drag. He was also the first person on the island to own a digital stopwatch. He had ordered it from a catalog and I remember it being incredibly expensive at the time. He always taught me that in order to achieve greatness you must push yourself beyond your comfort zone. That without pain, there is no gain. So if I complained after a swimming workout that my arms were sore, he would say: "Mari, the only way to excel in this sport is by training your thoughts to be stronger than your muscles. If you want the gold medals, go get them!" His dedication made it easier for me to endure the body aches and the chlorine, which stung my eyes and turned my hair green.

His mood on our drive home was dictated by how hard I'd worked at practice. The day he received the stopwatch, he and my coach reprimanded me more than once because instead of practicing for an upcoming meet, I was goofing off in the pool with my friends. My father ended up smashing his brand-new stopwatch against the ground, and I remember watching the springs fly in different directions. In the next event, I not only raced my best, but set a record in the fifty-meter backstroke for my age group. My father was bursting with pride and I thought I had finally pleased the man who always challenged me to do more.

The next morning, we were back at practice at five a.m., and before I jumped in the pool, he took his old, white-faced analog stopwatch out of his bag.

"This," he said, dangling the watch in front of me, "is your new rival."

I can still see him standing there at the pool's edge, with that analog stopwatch *tick-tick-ticking* as it hung from a lanyard around his neck. This was our time together. More than anything, swimming was how we came to the table, how a driven father and his competitive daughter channeled a passion that bonded them.

In the spring of 1971, I earned a spot on the Puerto Rican junior national team for the Central American Games in Havana, Cuba. My mother went with me, since my father could not abandon the university for two entire weeks. I was eleven and it was the first time I traveled overseas for a competition. My girlfriends and I were so excited to be there that at night, we had pillow fights and stayed up talking, sometimes until dawn.

I earned three medals: one gold, one silver, and one bronze. But when my father heard the results, he was so disappointed that he didn't even come to the airport to pick up my mother and me.

I joke with him now that in today's society that would have been considered child abuse. Looking back, as hurt as I was by his absence, I understood deep down why he was so upset. He didn't show up that day because he knew I had everything I needed to win three gold medals. I was in great shape and my times in practice were superb; he knew that if I didn't bring home all gold, it was because I had not followed the plan.

And he was right. Those late nights chatting with my girlfriends caught up with me, affecting my performance at the races. Understandably, he was disappointed that I had lost my focus and not given my maximum effort. He always wanted me to shoot higher, not for him but for myself. If I was the best in my town, he challenged me to be the best in my country, then the best in Central America, and then in the world.

I suffered a bigger disappointment at fifteen when I qualified for the 1976 Olympics in Montreal, Canada. I spent the previous year, my junior year of high school, boarding at Pine Crest Preparatory School in Fort Lauderdale, Florida, training for the ultimate competition. But three weeks before I was set to go to Canada, I caught mononucleosis, the "kissing disease." Ironically, I was a late bloomer and had not yet even kissed a boy. I was devastated as I watched the opening ceremony from my bed, my Olympic team uniform hanging in the closet.

But my father was, overall, incredibly upbeat and couldn't have been more proud of me. I had given my maximum effort and it was only something beyond my control that kept me from my goal.

I could have competed again in the 1979 Pan American Games and probably won a gold medal, but I didn't feel compelled to swim competitively after Montreal, not for my father, not for myself. Even though I had thoroughly enjoyed swimming, life called me to new challenges, new goals, and new experiences. And I chased them the way my father taught me, with relentless tenacity, challenging myself and never settling for "good enough." Every time a new challenge plagued me with doubts or fears, I replaced hesitation with the mental countdown that I had used to jump into the pool, and just as it helped me succeed as a competitive swimmer when I was a child, it still spurs me in the right direction.

When I was about to make my debut in television in my mid-twenties, I felt a paralyzing mixture of excitement and nerves. Fight or flight is how scientists define the biological response to extreme stress. The thought was daunting—my palms were sweaty and my heart was racing. But just as I had done when facing a frigid pool, I used the studio manager's countdown, *Three . . . two . . . one . . .* as I dove into this new endeavor. That discipline of mind over body served me well and continues to do so today. It wasn't by accident that I became a Central American champion swimmer by age ten, or that I qualified for the Olympics before turning sixteen. Nor that in 2006 I was chosen to appear on the cover of *Newsweek* as one of the most powerful women of my generation, or that I became the first Hispanic journalist to receive an Emmy Award.

When I got my first big job offer in New York, when I decided to adopt a child, when I was asked to cohost the *Today* show for the first time and I was worried about my accent—in every instance where others might have been bogged down with all the potential roadblocks, I did as my father taught me since elementary school: I jumped in wholeheartedly.

There is never an end of the road when it comes to personal achievement. My father always laid out a new challenge, the way life often does in the real world. I thank him for preparing me.

I will never forget those mornings by the pool, the smell

of chlorine in the air, and I can still hear that stopwatch *tick-tick-ticking* in my head. My father was right: Anybody can be good, but it takes discipline and hard work to accomplish great things. I was fortunate to be blessed with such a wonderful cheerleader, but I realize he's not always going to be around. In the end, all we have is ourselves. And like my dad said, your toughest rival should be you.

3

PEOPLE ARE NEITHER GOOD NOR BAD, JUST PRODUCTS OF CIRCUMSTANCE.

We all have a tendency to look at the world in terms of black and white, when the world is actually a quilt of shades of gray.

The moment we come to terms with this concept, our horizons open up and we get a much better understanding of others and of ourselves. Looking back, I came to terms with this in 2003 during an interview with Humberto Zurita, a very talented Mexican actor, in his Miami apartment.

At the time, he was the villain in a popular Telemundo *telenovela* called *Thief of Hearts.* When I mentioned how evil I thought his character was, he gave me a reply that was perplexing and profound and has stayed with me for years:

"People are neither good nor bad," he said. "People act according to circumstance."

I thought about his comment on the way home. I thought about all the times I had drawn a line and labeled people "good" or "bad." *How many times had I rushed to judge someone harshly?*

And then I thought of Ada Perkins.

We were both teenagers in Puerto Rico, she a year older than I, when we both liked the same boy: Pedro.

Back then, when my girlfriends and I wanted to go to the disco, we would tell our parents that we were headed to the big debutante events and would get all dressed up in our long puffy dresses that looked like wedding cakes. To keep up the charade, we would ask a friend who my parents considered a "serious boy" to pick us up at home. As soon as he arrived in his car, we would toss a bag with our makeup, blouses, and miniskirts to him out the second-floor window. We would then drive to the nearby Burger King and change into our party clothes to hit the San Juan clubs.

On those nights, I frequently ran into Pedro, and he would ask me out. But I initially kept my distance because I was told he was dating Ada Perkins. He denied it over and over, until he finally convinced me and I agreed to go out with him.

Pedro took me to a club for our date and he started showing off right away. He bought champagne for all my friends who stopped by our table to say hello. It was the first time someone bought me champagne.

Dom Perignon, no less.

With his dad's credit card, no less.

Again, he insisted he didn't have a girlfriend, and I let my guard down enough to fall for him further. He gave me his wristwatch and I wore it proudly, as a symbol that we were officially a couple.

That night, Pedro got in a lot of trouble.

After he dropped me off, he got into a fight and ended up with a broken hand, and his father found a copy of the bill with charges for all the bottles of champagne.

That should have been a warning sign right there, but I got sidetracked when I heard he had surgery on his hand and was convalescing at home. A friend convinced me I should pay him a visit—not that I needed much convincing.

She drove me to his house, and while she waited in the car I built up the courage to knock on the door.

I was about to knock again when the door opened. It was Ada Perkins. We had a couple of girlfriends in common, but there was nothing friendly about her that afternoon.

"What are *you* doing here?" she asked with a sense of authority that would have led anyone to believe she owned both Pedro and the house.

"I came to see how Pedro is doing," I said, wanting to flee for my life and trying to sound sarcastic and secure, like her. "And what are *you* doing here, playing nurse?"

"No," she responded. "I'm here as his girlfriend."

Okay, I really wasn't expecting that response, and I would have been more than happy if the earth, in pity, had swallowed me whole. To add insult to injury, she asked me in to meet Pedro's mother. I don't remember what excuse I gave her to avoid further embarrassment, but I left with my tail between my legs before I could suffer any further humiliation.

From that day on, every time I ran into her it was very . . . unpleasant. She would stare at me with narrowed hazel eyes, and if looks could kill, I'd have been dead on the spot. She had a nasty attitude, I decided, and I instantly labeled *her* the "bad one." (Never mind Pedro, who had lied to us both.)

Our mutual contempt lasted for a couple of years—way after she broke up with Pedro and was crowned Miss Puerto Rico in 1978, way after I dated him a couple more times in college and lost interest. He was out of the picture, yet Ada and I held a grudge.

Then something unexpected happened.

I was home from college the summer of my twentieth birthday, celebrating the birthday of one of my friends at a San Juan club, when I noticed the front door swing open and a mane of blond hair make its way through. Ada walked in looking more gorgeous than ever. Yet this time I didn't feel that rush to puff my feathers like a rooster in a cockfight. Instead, I felt an unexplainable desire to instantly bury the hatchet. I got up from my chair and walked over to her, and the smile that appeared on my face came straight from my heart.

"Hi, Ada, how are you?" I said, extending an open hand and leaning in to kiss her on the cheek, as is our custom.

She took my hand, smiled, and kissed me back. She said she was glad to see me, too.

I walked back to my friends that night feeling a sense of relief and liberation, that something out of balance was right again.

The next morning, when I unfolded the newspaper, I saw a picture of Ada Cecille Perkins Flores on the front page. And next to it, a picture of wreckage. Ada had been killed in a car accident after she left the club that night with her boyfriend, who, the story said, had been driving under the influence.

She was twenty-one years old.

That last meeting was my last chance. Our last chance. And I feel deep inside that it was no coincidence. I know that had I not taken the opportunity to make peace with Ada, although it was over something trivial, I would have regretted it for the rest of my life. Her memory reminds me that holding on to grudges and resentment means choosing to carry those burdens.

On the night I last saw Ada Perkins alive, I chose to move through life without that weight. When she took my hand, I think she did the same, and I learned an important lesson about judging others.

I like to think we both would have agreed that neither one of us was bad, after all.

Rest in peace, Ada.

4

IN TIMES OF TROUBLE, HOLD ON TO YOUR INTEGRITY.

It is during the worst of circumstances that we discover what a person is made of. Sometimes our image of that person crumbles. At other times we realize that that person is made of stuff we never imagined. And that is when our admiration grows.

It was during my first year of marriage to Guillermo Ramis that I learned one of the most important lessons about integrity and perseverance. When I met Guillermo he was the owner of the advertising agency where I worked. I know what you're thinking. The fact is I worked there for more than a year before either of us saw the other as more than a coworker.

He was experienced, a man sixteen years my senior, and I was a twenty-three-year-old still trying to find direction. Guillermo was knowledgeable and self-confident, worlds apart from the young men I had so far met. I marveled at his intellect, his grace, his generosity. He read thirty magazines a month from cover to cover and could speak to anyone about any subject in detail.

One night, after an office party, he and I stayed after the others left. Over a glass of wine we talked for the first time about our lives and aspirations. Something shifted between us. I no longer saw him only as a businessman I admired, but also as a man. A man I could love. A year later, we were married, and it was shortly after that that I truly saw his ability to deal with things that were out of his control.

His advertising agency was coasting along, firm in its dealings with stable clients who trusted Guillermo's work completely. Things were so good that he decided to buy out his partner and expand the company.

And then the unthinkable happened.

One of Guillermo's main clients went out of business, leaving a quarter of a million dollars in unpaid debts. It was a tremendous blow, especially considering that Guillermo had just taken out a loan to pay his former partner. In spite of this, he had a solid roster of clients, including a major airline that had just written his firm a check for $150,000.

And then one of its planes went down.

"Thank God they paid me $150,000 the day before the plane crash," Guillermo told me. "Otherwise, we would have crashed with them!"

Two days later, that check bounced.

The airline filed for bankruptcy, owing Guillermo a little over $500,000. As if that weren't enough, that same month, another one of his major clients, a local supermarket chain that owed him $250,000, filed for Chapter 11. Guillermo's company faced a similar fate. It seemed too awful to be true.

Young and inexperienced in that world, I lost sleep, paced the hallways, worried for my husband. But Guillermo never lost his composure.

"When one owes money, the worst thing you can do is hide. The correct thing to do is to assume your responsibilities," he would say.

Guillermo could have blown off his creditors by filing for bankruptcy. He could have left the country and started over somewhere else. But it was a matter of honor; his name and reputation were at stake, and because I was his wife, so were mine. So he stayed and faced the situation like a man. Even though he was emotionally distraught, he put on a brave face and explained to his employees that, regretfully, he had to let them go. Since the company was in the red, he paid each and every one of them their last paycheck, including vacation time and benefits, from his own pocket.

That night he came home and we curled up on the couch. I was both proud of him and worried for our future. It was tough for Guillermo to accept that he had failed at something to which he had dedicated so much of his life. Yet his concern was not how *he* was going to overcome this financial crisis, but the devastating effect it could have on the small vendors that could go under if his company didn't pay what was owed to them. He thought of the three brothers who owned the small printing shop, the handyman, and the mom-and-pop messenger service that had served the agency for so many years, and vowed that he would pay them first, no matter what.

Guillermo hired an accountant at his own expense to make sure that all monies still owed to the company were paid. And when the first checks arrived, true to his word, he paid every cent he owed to the independent contractors and small businesses. He then met with all his big creditors and asked them to work out payment plans so that he could meet his financial obligations in a reasonable manner. Some of them threatened to sue. Most of them, though, because of his long, honorable history, gave him a break.

Guillermo dealt with legal matters that left my head spinning, but he tackled each problem with aplomb. "All we can do is start all over again like my parents had to do when they left Cuba after the Communist revolution, with only the clothes on their backs," he said.

In the midst of all the turmoil we had no choice but to continue servicing our clients. If we didn't, we ran the risk of losing them to the competing agencies that, knowing of our near demise, were circling them like sharks. It was chaotic. While our office was being dismantled because we couldn't pay the rent and the furniture was being sold, the phone wouldn't stop ringing. I had to field the daily phone calls from the unhappy creditors demanding immediate payment and the clients expecting their deadlines to be met. Everyone was calling except our so-called friends.

Thank God for family. My father lent us a small space in a building he owned and we moved the office there. With the help of some freelancers and through sheer determination and hard work the business eventually took off again. We survived against all odds, because we formed a solid front as a couple and as business partners.

Guillermo had been on the brink of losing everything, yet none of his major clients abandoned him. On the contrary, after seeing how he faced adversity with such integrity, their respect for him deepened. Just as mine did.

To this day, he's still at the helm of the advertising agency that, for a second time, he built from scratch. He is still a successful businessman because he never burned a bridge.

The "friends" who had so conveniently kept their distance also returned, but by then we understood the difference between those who stand by you and those who stand with you.

My parents always taught me that money can't be the pillar of your life, because it comes and goes. They believe that when you lose everything, your true character is tested. And that through it all, you must have faith in yourself, believe in your talent, and act according to your principles.

Whether you believe in God, fate, or karma, the Universe has a long memory. Give it a good reason to treat you gently.

5

BETTER TO BE THE HEAD OF A MOUSE THAN THE TAIL OF A LION.

Sometimes life dangles a carrot in front of us to see if we'll bite, to gauge whether our hunger is capable of blinding us. Many people choose to eat the carrot and fail to discover the banquet that lies behind it.

I faced that temptation during my first job in journalism, a job I was offered when no one else would hire a young communications major with no experience. Yet my loyalty was tested early on, with a carrot so sweet, and so hard to resist.

Fresh out of college, I returned to Puerto Rico to begin my career as a journalist, only to find myself, like so many other recent college graduates, stonewalled at the local television stations. There were few jobs available, and even fewer for someone just out of college. All the jobs required some previous experience, yet I could not get that experience without first having a job. It was a frustrating catch-22.

I ended up working as a copywriter for Guillermo's advertising agency. At the beginning it was a lot of fun. I would spend my days in the fantastic world of the creative department, where everyone was artistic or intellectual or both. I loved being around the creative director, the other copywriters, and the graphic artists, analyzing the human mind, having existential conversations, and coming up with crazy concepts. But mostly I enjoyed their jokes when a client wouldn't get the genius marketing campaigns we came up with.

From day one Guillermo had great faith in my potential, and when he saw that I was a hard worker and smart, he quickly promoted me to account executive in charge of his most important clients. He made sure I learned everything about the business, and I lived to make him proud of me. He was a great teacher and I was an eager student. But I missed the intellectual stimulation from the creative part of the business, and I didn't like having to deal with clients and their daily whims.

The truth is that I always yearned to follow my true calling, which was journalism. My dream was to be an eyewitness to the historic events of my time, to report on and denounce the injustices of the world, to make a difference—not having to cater to clients. Yes, I was good at the job, but not great, not in love with the work. I thought about my father, who so often lectured me about getting an A or an F but never to settle for being average. I felt like I was selling my soul, but I stuck it out because at least advertising was an industry related to my field. The chances of my coming across an interesting opportunity were greater at the agency than if I were to stay at home.

And finally, it paid off. At an advertising award ceremony, I met an entrepreneur who wanted to start a twenty-four-hour news station on the island and was looking for young anchors and reporters. The candidates had to meet only two requirements: They needed to have a journalism degree, and they had to be willing to work long hours for meager pay. I met both criteria. I was one of those people with drive and no bad habits, someone he could mold.

To my dismay, the next morning I discovered that I was

one of more than four hundred applicants, but after three grueling interviews, I got the job. About fifty of us became part of what turned out to be a magical moment in the island's broadcasting history. With Channel 24, we brought the world news to Puerto Rico from the perspective of its own people, before the local stations traveled abroad to cover stories. Our group of rookies took the island by storm, with sheer enthusiasm and a love for news. I traveled so much in only four months that I got enough miles to become a member of the American Airlines Platinum Club.

In my new job as anchor and reporter, I was at my best doing live coverage. Everyone started to notice me.

That's when the call came—enter the dangling carrot.

One of the television stations I had interviewed with when I returned to Puerto Rico—the most-watched on the island—called to offer me a job. The same station manager who had given me the runaround when I first applied for a job was now willing to triple my salary. And his more established station had an audience three times bigger than my current employer.

Most people would have jumped at the offer or used it as leverage for a raise at Channel 24. But I never considered either option. I felt gratitude toward my boss because he had bet on me when no one else would. I felt privileged to cover stories all over the world. Going to another local station would have meant giving up that opportunity in order to report on the usual fare of car crashes and water main breaks that shut down traffic. I would have to go from being a lead anchor on the smaller Channel 24 to the end of the line of field reporters at the larger station.

It made me think of an old Spanish phrase: *"Mejor ser cabeza de ratón que cola de león"*—"Better to be the head of a mouse than the tail of a lion."

I turned down the offer and never told anyone about it. Some of my colleagues would have called it a crazy decision. I called it poetic justice.

A few weeks later, with the industry being so small, word got back to my boss, and he called me into his office. He had heard about the offer and about my loyalty. And although he couldn't match the money, he gave me what I needed more than anything in my life: a new challenge. He said he wanted to reward me by giving me one of the most coveted assignments at the time: covering the Soviet Union as it began opening up to the world.

That trip to the USSR earned me the Journalist of the Year award, bestowed by the Puerto Rican Chamber of Commerce. During the awards ceremony, I managed to get an exclusive interview with the featured speaker, Reverend Jesse Jackson, who at the time was aspiring to become the Democratic Party's presidential nominee. One of the many journalists present at the event was so impressed, a few months later he offered me a job in New York and the chance to enter the very important Hispanic market in the United States.

This time, I did approach my boss at Channel 24, and he agreed that this was the opportunity of a lifetime. With his blessing, I accepted the offer.

All of our actions have a reaction. Each of our decisions has the power to push us away or get us closer to the plan the Universe has in store for us. In this case, having done the correct thing rather than being driven by greed unleashed a set of events that took me right where I needed to be.

You will always have temptation from some tasty-looking carrot. But never let it blind you to the feast that awaits just beyond it.

6

WHERE OTHERS SEE OBSTACLES, YOU CAN FIND OPPORTUNITIES.

It came as a reward and a challenge all at once.

When my boss at Channel 24 told me I was going to the Soviet Union, I'm sure I was still bouncing out of his office, still turning to thank him, thrilled at my good fortune, when it all started settling over me like, well, like an Iron Curtain. I had one of the greatest assignments any reporter in the West could dream of. There was just one little problem: getting in.

It was the summer of 1987, shortly after the Soviet government announced a series of historic reforms for the Soviet Union that would open the country to the rest of the world. Countless reporters wanted to travel to the USSR and document this new era of glasnost and perestroika, reform and openness, but only a few were allowed in. Even for the big networks with their teams of producers and consultants, getting access was a challenge, and here I was, all by myself, figuring out how to go about it. I had something of a Rubik's cube in front of me: How in the world do you get into Russia?

I went to my husband, Guillermo, for advice. He was a businessman who had traveled extensively and seemed to have a formula for handling any situation. We decided the best course of action was to put all our cards on the table and contact the Soviet government directly.

Over the next few days, we crafted an exhaustive, three-page letter that detailed every aspect of the stories I wanted to do in Moscow for Channel 24. I had not written an outline so complete since college. And we pumped up the prestige of the station, calling it the only twenty-four-hour news network in the Caribbean. When we were done, we felt confident that all the questions that could be asked had been addressed, and my story wish list was complete.

The only way to send my letter to the Ministry of Communications and Media in the USSR was via telex, the precursor of the fax machine, which typed out messages on a dot-matrix printer. It cost a fortune to send. And I waited.

And waited.

And waited some more, for a full two months, until a telex came from Moscow in response. It *clack-clack-clacked* away and my heart sank as I read it. I don't remember the exact wording, but the gist of it was this: "We get a hundred requests like yours every day. Forget it, Channel 24."

I showed it to Guillermo. I was devastated. He was chipper.

"Don't give up, Mari," he said. "There has to be a way around it."

He looked at the date on the telex. It was October, the month in which Soviets celebrated the victory of the Bolshevik revolution. The answer became crystal clear to him.

We replied with just two perfect sentences: "Congratulations, comrades, on the anniversary of the revolution. Please reconsider our request."

This time we didn't have to wait long. In less than two weeks we got a response: "Prepare to arrive in Moscow on December 10. . . ." I couldn't believe it. It had been a brilliant move on Guillermo's part. As much as he despised Communists, he knew that flattery will get you anywhere.

I spent ten days in the Soviet Union in the dead of winter with my cameraman, running in and out of our car to film segments in below-zero temperatures. I was writer, producer, lighting engineer, and general gofer extraordinaire. But we got to do everything we wanted and more. I got unprecedented access to the headquarters of the infamous Soviet intelligence agency, the KGB, and in Leningrad I had an exclusive interview with Dr. Svyatoslav Fyodorov, the ophthalmologist who developed the revolutionary vision correction procedure known as radial keratotomy. I also spent a whole day with a typical Moscow family and documented their hardships. They took me to a supermarket, where after waiting in line for hours people left empty-handed because there was nothing to buy. I was granted special permission to film inside the Soviet Space Center, where we established communication with the cosmonauts aboard the space station *Mir.* Live from outer space the cosmonauts wished my viewers in Puerto Rico a Merry Christmas. When the one-hour holiday special *A Puerto Rican in Moscow* aired a few days later, it was a total hit and my career took off.

I also learned a lesson in persistence: One should not get discouraged when confronted with obstacles, even if they seem as impenetrable as the Iron Curtain. Behind every obstacle, there is an opportunity. You just have to look for it with an iron will.

7

WHEN YOUR DIGNITY IS AT STAKE, ALWAYS STAND YOUR GROUND.

I never set out to make headlines in Seoul.

But it just so happens that a woman—a foreigner, for that matter—had never spoken to a man in a position of power the way I had to the representative of South Korea's Ministry of Sports. It was a lesson for both of us. But I think he learned his lesson more sharply.

In the spring of 1988, I spent several weeks reporting for Puerto Rico's Channel 24 on a series of stories that took me from Hawaii to the Philippines to the Marshall Islands in the Pacific. Since the summer Olympics were approaching in that part of the world, I figured it would be a good time to do a piece from the host country, South Korea.

Before I met with the representative of the Ministry of Sports, I had heard the warnings. Women have traditional roles in that society, and for me to sit him down for an interview might be a little, well, tense. Plus, I was told to expect him to speak to me only in Korean since their language is a source of national pride.

I was pleasantly surprised when, upon entering his office, he greeted my cameraman in fluent English and with a firm handshake. I sat across from him and the camera started rolling. Right from the start, I realized there were two major problems: He stopped speaking English, and he refused to look at me. Watching the tape, you'd think his English was a problem. Or that he was camera shy. You'd be wrong on both counts.

I am not sure whether he was trying to prove a point, or maintain a social norm, but he continued to ignore me even after I asked him to acknowledge me. Each time I asked a question he would direct his answer, in Korean, to my cameraman, as if I were invisible. This went on for more than five minutes. And, oh, how long those minutes are when you feel them stoking your fury as they pass. I tried one more time, this time more tersely:

"Either you look at me and answer me directly, in English, or we're leaving," I warned him.

He fell silent, still looking away.

I asked another question and waited.

He picked up where he'd left off, as if his ludicrous monologue in this ridiculous movie had been paused and then resumed.

I tapped my cameraman on the shoulder and put my hand over the lens.

"We're done here," I said, and started toward the door. "I'm not taking this anymore."

And I wasn't bluffing. We had traveled from the other side of the globe, but I was willing to pack up and leave rather than submit to this humiliation any longer.

When I turned to see if my cameraman was following, I saw the government official sitting there with an incredulous look on his face. It was hard to tell whether he was in shock because this young, redheaded Puerto Rican woman had given him an ultimatum, or because she had followed through with her threat.

Whatever it was, I gave him one last chance: "Are you going to speak in English . . . to *me*?" Surprisingly, he nodded, the way a child does after being reprimanded.

We started from scratch, with him answering in fluent English and making a genuine effort to look me in the eye. At the end, I left with a great interview and my head held high.

Long after I returned to San Juan, I heard that the story of our miniature cold war made news in the newspapers and on television back in Seoul. Since I don't speak or read Korean, I can't tell you who came off as the villain. And frankly, I don't care if it was me. I only demanded the same respect from the government official that he demanded from anybody else. Dignity is nonnegotiable.

8

IF YOU WANT TO GO PLACES, DON'T LET THE WORD "NO" STAND IN YOUR WAY.

One word in the English language has more power than any other: the word "no."

It is one of the first words we learn as babies, and it shapes our lives every step of the way.

Sometimes it keeps us out of trouble. But other times, it keeps us from our goals.

I have always felt that "no" comes as a natural first

reaction to many people. And so I have refused to accept it as a final answer. It's something I learned during the 1988 U.S. presidential primaries.

Civil rights activist Jesse Jackson was little known to the American public when he ran for the Democratic presidential bid in 1984. Yet by 1988 he gave Massachusetts governor Michael Dukakis a run for his money, winning six states and the Puerto Rico caucus. But in the summer of that year, as the Democratic National Convention approached, Dukakis began running away with the electoral votes, and it seemed only a matter of time before the man who blazed a trail as the first serious African-American presidential hopeful conceded defeat. The news media followed Jackson to every campaign stop, every function, every meeting with supporters and dignitaries: They all wanted to be there when he made the inevitable announcement ending his campaign.

It was then that I first met Jesse Jackson.

He came to speak at an annual banquet hosted by the Puerto Rican Chamber of Commerce, where I was being honored as Journalist of the Year for my work about life in the Soviet Union. We sat at the same enormous table, about a mile apart. They had cordoned off the area, and on the other side of the rope were journalists from the major networks and wire services in the United States—from CNN and the Associated Press to all the local media. Everyone wanted just a second with Jackson, enough to find out whether he had already worked out a deal with the Dukakis campaign to concede the nomination. They had all been told he was off-limits to the media. Channel 24 was no exception.

I decided to give it a shot anyway, and approached his press manager with confidence. "I just wanted to know at what time you have me scheduled to interview Mr. Jackson," I said to her. She looked at me like I was crazy and told me the same thing she had already said to countless reporters and media organizations: No, Reverend Jackson would not be granting any interviews tonight.

"Oh, I see. But I don't know if you're aware that every year the Journalist of the Year interviews the speaker of the night. It's a tradition," I told her. "I think the best thing is for you to talk to the director of the Chamber and let him know." This was not exactly true. And by that, I mean it was a total fabrication. But I figured it couldn't hurt.

I imagine she worried that her refusal to make her boss available to me might be interpreted as a slap in the face by the organizers of the event. She turned around, walked to Jackson and whispered something in his ear. He looked in my direction and I smiled.

The press secretary returned with her "no" replaced by a much more amenable response: "Fine," she told me. "You have ten minutes."

Reverend Jackson and I were whisked to a private room, as his security detail held off other reporters who tried to follow us. They complained—loudly. The news director of one of the largest radio networks on the island, Christopher Crommett, was one of the most vocal protesters. He wanted to know why the Jackson campaign was giving me preferential treatment.

That was not the last time I heard from Christopher Crommett. Three months later he called me to share the news that he had been named news director of the Univision affiliate in New York. He said that he had been impressed by my ability to finagle an interview with Reverend Jackson, and that he was looking for a fearless and aggressive journalist, just like me. He was considering me for a job. But not just any job. It was a position that would introduce me to the U.S. Hispanic market.

Thinking back, I realize that I could have accepted the

initial "no" from Jackson's press secretary. It would have been easy to turn around and just enjoy the party. After all, It was my big night. Yet I chose to chase the interview and it paid off.

Very often people will try to dismiss you with a simple "no." But if you truly want to advance in your career, don't take it as a final answer. Just try again and erase the word "no" from your vocabulary.

9

EVEN YOUR MISTAKES CAN SHOW THE BEST OF YOU.

When I heard the phone in my hotel room ringing, I had no idea the person on the other end of the line was calling to change my life.

It rang just as I was about to open the door. I was dressed in cold-weather gear and it rang and I wrestled to pull off my gloves so that I could look for the key in my pocket. It rang and I dropped my ski poles. It rang as I opened the door. It rang for the last time, and I almost missed it.

Out of breath, I picked it up on the last ring just in time to hear a voice I did not expect, much less while on a ski vacation in Vail, Colorado, with my husband, Guillermo.

It was Christopher Crommett, the same Christopher Crommett who just three months before had complained loudly when I landed the exclusive interview with Jesse Jackson. He was now in charge of the news department of Channel 41 in New York, an affiliate of Univision.

"That night I said to myself that if I ever had the chance, I would hire you for my team," he told me over the phone, and then offered me the anchor job at his new station. It was the break I was looking for.

Although he was convinced of my talent, he needed to show his boss, the station's general manager, a sample of my work to prove to him that I had what it took. I promised to send my highlight tape, something I had ready for just such an occasion. I had spent endless hours in the editing room, splicing together the best pieces of my best reporting from across the globe. When I was done, I was sure I had captured the best of me in magnetic tape. He needed the tape immediately, and although I was not home, I promised to come through.

I called a reporter friend of mine back at Channel 24 and

asked her to put it in the mail. I spent the rest of that vacation on a high, hoping the tape would seal the deal.

When I returned to the office about a week later, I was going through my files . . . and I came across my highlight tape. But if it was here, which tape, dear God, had made its way to New York?

I rushed to my friend, tape in hand.

"That's the one you wanted to send?" she answered, her eyes wide.

"Which one did you send?" I asked, feeling sweat beginning to bead on my brow.

We went rushing back into my office and she pointed to the spot where another tape had been.

Oh, no . . . not that one!

Instead of my video résumé, she had sent a tape of me repeating the intro to a news story over and over. A blooper reel, if you will. I looked like a fool, and if Crommett showed that tape to his station manager, he would think Crommett was an even bigger fool.

I called Christopher immediately, hoping the tape had been lost in the mail. Or that maybe he hadn't had a chance to show it to his boss, and I could convince him to wait for the right one. But before I could explain away the mix-up, he said he had received the tape, and I felt my knees go weak.

His boss had already seen the tape—and had liked it very much, in fact. He thought it gutsy that, instead of a highlight reel, I had sent raw footage of myself, determined to get the intro to a story just right. It showed my tenacity, my dedication to excellence, he said, and that's just what his station needed.

That, more than anything else, was the reason he asked Christopher to offer me the job, right there and then.

I did eventually send them the correct highlight tape, but I doubt they bothered to watch it.

I learned a valuable lesson from my faux pas: Even when others catch you with your guard down, they should see the same person as when you are at your very best.

10

SOUR LEMONS MAKE THE BEST LEMONADE.

I arrived in New York ready to take on the world.

In only two years as a television journalist in Puerto Rico, I had accomplished more than other reporters on the island had achieved in their entire lifetimes. I had excelled in the media industry back home, and there was no doubt in my mind that in this vibrant city I would do the same. It seemed that there was no challenge I couldn't meet, and I was eager to have the

Big Apple for lunch. Little did I know that *I* would turn out to be the main course.

I came in ready to work as the main news anchor of Univision's local affiliate in the largest media market in the country. I was as excited as can be—until I saw the ad campaign that the station's marketing department had created to introduce me to viewers. It was way over-the-top and flattering, but it made me apprehensive.

It went against one of the most important lessons I learned during my days as a swimmer: underplay your talents, then pleasantly surprise. I knew right off the bat that this fabulous campaign was going to backfire. And it sure did.

Sooner than I thought.

From the moment I arrived in the station's newsroom, I felt unwelcome. I could feel the resentment behind the carefully rehearsed smiles. Promoting me as a megastar had only served to prejudice my coworkers against me. *No one could be that good.* They knew that it was almost impossible for anyone to live up to such high expectations. And they were going to make sure I didn't.

The attacks began my first week on the job. They said I looked too young to be a credible newscaster and they made fun of my Puerto Rican accent. The assignment editor was a

Colombian woman named Janneth Quintero. She spoke very beautiful Spanish and her enunciation was perfect, unlike mine. She would go around forecasting that I was going to alienate the viewers of other Spanish-speaking countries with my thick accent and poor diction.

I knew I had a baby face and a heavy accent, but after such a meteoric career move, I was self-assured. I felt that I had other redeeming values and the capacity to overcome any shortcomings. So, at first, I didn't give it much thought.

Then came the scrutiny about the way I dressed. And that took me by surprise. Upon arriving in New York I had gone shopping with a dear friend who is a fashion guru, and she helped me pick out a few key pieces of clothing so that I could mix and match. I ended up buying three suits, a couple of skirts, and a bunch of shirts. *More than enough,* I thought, naïve as I was. By the time I had repeated the suits, some of my coworkers started to spread the rumor that the switchboard operator couldn't handle the barrage of calls from viewers complaining about my limited wardrobe.

Whether it was true or not, I was hurt. For the first time I became keenly aware that people were not just listening to the reporting, they were studying every aspect of my image and personality. Up until then, I had focused all of my energy on the content of the newscast. Substance over style—isn't that how it is supposed to be? It was a warning sign of things to come.

Despite these challenges, those first three months went by fast and with relatively few problems, compared to what I was about to experience. I came into the office one morning to find that the general manager of the station, who had hired both Crommett and me, was leaving the company. Soon after, Crommett also left. It was tough to lose their support while I was still acclimating to the feeding frenzy of New York.

Within his first month, my new boss, whom I'll call Octavio, replaced fifteen of the thirty employees on staff with his own people. Then, one afternoon, half an hour before I was set to go on the air, I was sitting in the newsroom going over my notes when I heard a commotion from the other end of the room.

"I'm *baaaack*!" came a voice I recognized.

I poked my head over the cubicles.

It was the anchor I had replaced, a ten-year veteran. Octavio had rehired her. As I went down to the studio, embarrassed and humiliated, I could hear the cheers in the background. It took all my self-discipline to concentrate and get through that newscast, suspecting that it would be my last.

That night, I called my first husband, Guillermo, in

Puerto Rico and told him what had happened. I felt adrift, like a rudderless boat, sailing along without direction. If I sounded discouraged, he was the model of clear thinking. "Like him or not," Guillermo told me, "this news director is supposed to be experienced in his field. I'm sure he understands what it takes to make a good newscast, a good journalist. If I were you I would stay and learn from him instead of scurrying back to Puerto Rico."

I decided to stay and fight. And I would prove to Octavio, to my new coworkers, to myself, that I was not above listening to criticism. "And if you ever do end up leaving, it will be much easier to get a new job if you already have a job," Guillermo added. There's no doubt why Guillermo has been one of the strongest and most important influences in my life.

Octavio called me into his office the next morning. He sat smugly across from me with his arms crossed as he laid out my options. "You will not be the anchor any longer," he told me flatly. I had two choices: go home and receive my paycheck during the three years left on my contract, or stay and play by his rules. Most anchors, with their egos battered at this point, would have taken the buyout in their contract and moved on. I didn't.

"You've been handed a bag of lemons," he told me. "Now, you can suck sour lemons. Or you can make lemonade."

I thought I understood what he meant: Will you be able to make the best of a bad situation? I presumed that was his point. That day, in my eagerness to show my boss that I was a team player and that I was willing to swallow my pride, I searched what seemed like every drugstore and every stationery store in all of New York, looking for the perfect greeting card, one with a picture of lemons on the cover. Inside the blank card I wrote simply, "Let's make lemonade."

The next morning, I went into his office early, a smile curling beneath my lips, amused at my wittiness as I placed the card, along with a mesh bag full of lemons, on his desk. I was sure it would melt his hardened heart. But he never even acknowledged that he received it. That's when I understood the meaning of his little quip. To him, making lemonade meant taking the cash and knowing when I wasn't wanted. If he had truly been sincere about making it work between us, he certainly acted like he hadn't expected me to take him up on his offer. But I had made my decision and was ready to stand by it.

My husband's words rang in my head whenever it seemed I couldn't take more abuse—and those times came fast and furious. Octavio hired new reporters, many from radio who had never worked in television, and put them all in line ahead of me for every story. Most days I would stay at the office with nothing to do, while the new reporters and their cameramen went out to cover the news. Octavio wanted me to feel like an outsider. He even asked me to move out of my office so that the new weatherman he hired could move in. The entire newsroom watched as I packed up my belongings and moved them to the tiny Formica counter that Octavio ordered built for me, facing a wall, with no phone and no typewriter. He wanted to prove a point, and, ultimately, he wanted me to quit.

For about six months, I went home to my lonely apartment, nuked hot dogs in the microwave, and lay in bed, staring at the ceiling, depressed, fighting the urge to get on the next plane home.

In order to be on camera I did whatever it took. I came up with investigative stories and special series and asked the cameramen to work overtime so that we could go out and do the interviews. Also, every time a reporter called in sick I would jump at the chance to take his or her place. Although I was given the most boring assignment on the schedule, I made sure that it turned out to be the most complete and provocative story at the end of the day.

I distinguished myself by reporting live from the scene—a skill I had honed working on the always-live Channel 24, where we learned to work our best under the most stressful circumstances. I worked with a voice coach and watched videos of myself over and over, paying particular attention to my pronunciation, until I morphed my accent into a more neutral Spanish.

None of this went unnoticed by my coworkers. They saw that I was not a fallen prima donna, but someone trapped by circumstance. When they saw how hard I worked, in spite of everything, they started to respect me as an equal. But the harder I worked, the more I succeeded, the more Octavio seemed to stew in the knowledge that he had not broken me. Yet I desperately wanted Octavio to like me, to give me a real chance.

One day Octavio's nemesis, the vice president of the news department for Univision Network, visited New York on business, and while at his hotel he happened to see me on TV presenting a story. He liked me on camera so much that he called me after the show to see if I could go to California immediately and anchor the national weekend newscast while their regular anchor was on vacation. Octavio hit the roof. Beyond climbing out from under his thumb, I had come into the good graces of his superior, the man who at one point had been his peer and who Octavio profoundly disliked. Now he had gone over Octavio's head by contacting me directly. I was in the middle of their power struggle. One of them was trying to bury me, and the other wanted to give me wings.

Before my national debut, I went to Barbara Walters's hair salon for a very expensive makeover. At my request the makeup artist gave me tips to make me look older, one of which was to apply blush just below my cheekbones, which had the effect of sharpening my chubby cheeks, giving them a more chiseled look. And then I bit the bullet and plunked down a chunk of my hard-earned money on a great on-camera outfit.

My national debut on Univision was celebrated with high fives from the staff afterward, and I was invited back as a regular weekend substitute. I could only imagine what this was doing to Octavio, who was so desperately trying to save face.

I returned to New York renewed and confident, with the same eagerness to please Octavio. But nothing had changed and he still tried to thwart my every move. It was with great reluctance that he sent me to cover the mayoral debate in the city. The journalist assigned to it fell sick, and I was the last-minute replacement. The next morning, one of my questions to the eventual winner and longtime mayor Ed Koch was quoted by *The New York Times.* Octavio was livid. The more I shined, the more obvious it became to everyone in the newsroom that his dislike had nothing to do with my professional performance. It was personal.

"This guy's on his way down, Mari," Guillermo would say. "And you are on your way up."

Still, I was eager for any kind of praise from Octavio. Praise that never came, because my determination to stay was a direct challenge to his authority. Octavio's anger was fueled by my coworkers, who suggested, then insisted, that he should use me more often, give me more challenging stories, more airtime. And I guess that was the last straw.

I came in one morning and Octavio called me into his office to tell me my contract had been terminated. I had never been fired from a job. He paid me what was in the buyout, turned his back, and sent me on my way without thanks or apologies. I never expected a warm farewell from Octavio, but I thought I deserved at least a respectful nod. However, he had served his purpose. He helped me learn about perseverance and self-reliance.

For the next two weeks I lived in New York without a

job, but with a haircut and wardrobe that could have belonged to Barbara Walters. And then the phone rang. California was calling. National news. This time the offer was to take over as the chief of the Los Angeles bureau, the most important one for Univision, and to become the official substitute anchor for the weekend national newscast. It was another big break.

A big break that would not have come had I chosen to suck lemons.

11

IF YOU CAN'T CLIMB OVER AN OBSTACLE, DIG A TUNNEL UNDER IT.

We were the last to arrive. The story was over. Or so it seemed.

Most of the Spanish-speaking and English-language newscasts had already descended on the tiny Arizona town after word spread that someone had dug a tunnel beneath the border to smuggle undocumented immigrants and narcotics. Film crews were set up all around the exit of the tunnel on the U.S. side, doing stand-up shots, live shots, prerecorded shots, basically leaving us to eat their dust in the Arizona sun. But I had not driven straight through from California to leave empty-handed. I have always thought there is more than one perspective to any problem, and more than one angle to any story. And so, too, there may be more than one entrance to every tunnel.

My cameraman and I drove our rental car across the border and found the tiny police station in charge of securing the tunnel on the Mexican side. Inside was the police official that Hollywood dramatizes in its movies. Weasel-thin with beady eyes. Lecherous. All he was missing was the wispy mustache to twist as he examined me like a side of beef.

In an effort to impress me, he showed me the evidence room where they kept all the drugs that his men had confiscated during recent operations. All the while he kept trying to hold my hand and put his arm around my waist. He then offered to give me a private tour of the mansion where the entrance to the tunnel was located. There was only one condition. I had to have lunch with him first. I said *my cameraman* and I would be happy to join him for lunch, and with that we followed him and his driver in their squad car to a local tavern.

He immediately ordered tequila shots for us and began

having one after another. After a while he got so wasted that he could no longer tell that I had stopped drinking after the first round.

"I'm going to show you something no one has seen," he slurred as he got into his car. His chauffeur led the way down a desolate road to a sprawling mansion behind a wrought-iron gate as we followed closely in our rental car.

He unlocked the door to the mansion and led us into a game room where, at the center, there was an ornate pool table. He flipped a switch and the entire pool table rose with a hydraulic hiss, revealing a vault that led to the entrance of the tunnel that went under the house and into U.S. territory.

My cameraman started filming the scene as the official revealed all the inside details of how the operation worked. I even made on-camera commentaries while sitting on top of the pool table. We filled two tapes with what I was sure was award-winning footage. And it would probably have ended that way had the chauffeur not gotten a call from one of the official's sons.

They, too, were officers. His deputies.

Within fifteen minutes the sons arrived with several deputies to find their father three sheets to the wind, and they started worrying about how this might look for the Mexican government. Their father had spilled the beans on a sensitive topic and they were trying to figure our how to get the secrets back into Pandora's box. The sons whisked the father away and several other deputies remained in their place. They stopped us from recording any further. While no one was looking, I grabbed one of the tapes from my bag and threw it over the fence into an undeveloped lot behind the house. Minutes later, one of the policemen asked me for all the tapes so they could be vetted by authorities. I handed over the only tape I had and was told that we were not allowed to leave while we waited for them to view the tape.

And so while we waited, the deputies raided the mansion's liquor cabinet, and began drinking. And drinking. Over the course of eight hours, we were held captive, my cameraman coming between me and the men who made passes at me, as the official had, with alcohol steaming from their breath. They commented on my looks, my figure, whether I was married, and, for the first time, I truly began to fear for my safety.

By the time the deputies were barely moving from their drunken stupor, my cameraman nudged me, mumbled something about getting cigarettes from the car, and we hurried quickly out the door. Before any of them could react, we hopped in the car, raced to the empty lot, opened the door enough to grab the tape off the ground while the car was still moving, and headed for the border. We had heard stories about Mexican officers coming across the border, and we didn't want to test our luck. So we left our clothes at the hotel in Arizona and drove straight to the Univision bureau in Los Angeles.

That night, footage of the hydraulic pool table covering the mouth of the tunnel aired on both Univision and ABC, a common practice of quid pro quo between the networks. I wasn't credited on air, but my bosses learned that I always delivered, no matter the obstacles.

There's a lesson here about how far to trust a Mexican border cop.

But it is not more important than learning to look at a difficult situation from a different point of view.

12

SOMETIMES A SIDE ROAD IS THE FASTEST PATH TO REACH YOUR GOALS. AND BEYOND.

No doubt about it, focusing on one's goals is essential to reaching them. But if we approach our goals with tunnel vision we may fail to see the endless possibilities around us that can take us further than we ever imagined. That's why it is so important to have an open mind and to recognize that what might seem like a roadblock may actually be a guide to a new and better direction.

I moved to Miami in 1991, when Univision relocated its headquarters from Laguna Niguel, California, to Florida. I was named national news weekend anchor and was busy doing what weekend anchors do: hustling, hustling, hustling to get face time during the week. For a span of three years, I volunteered to work every holiday—Thanksgiving, Christmas, New Year's Day, the Fourth of July, even my birthday—whenever one of the top two anchors was out. It was a sacrifice I was willing to make because I dreamed of one day anchoring the daily national newscast.

Even though María Elena Salinas and Jorge Ramos had been the main anchors for many years and had built excellent reputations, there was always the possibility that one of them would move on and an anchor position would become available. If that were to happen, I wanted to be the natural choice to replace them.

But it was not meant to be. María Elena and Jorge chose to renew their contracts with Univision for many years to come. That meant that I had two choices: stay as a frustrated weekend anchor and wait indefinitely, or shift gears and look for another opportunity.

While I was reassessing my goals, opportunity came knocking at my door, and at first, I didn't recognize it as such.

The Mexican media conglomerate Televisa became Univision's main partner, and corporate restructuring and programming changes took place at the network. In the middle of all the changes, word reached me that Myrka Dellanos, one of the coanchors of *Noticias y Más*, a Univision infotainment show, had come down with chicken pox. I was asked to fill in for two weeks.

This was not an easy decision. I had earned my stripes as a hardened journalist, covered civil unrest and politics, and in the process sacrificed my personal life to do so. Now I was being asked to coanchor a newsmagazine that aired mostly sensationalistic stories, scandals, and amazing videos. My biggest fear was that it would affect my credibility and eliminate any chance I had of one day sitting in María Elena's or Jorge's chair.

When I shared my predicament with my mother, she gave me great advice: "With all the changes at the network, this is no time for you to be difficult. I suggest that you do as they say. When in turbulent waters, don't rock the boat!"

So I accepted and, to my surprise, I loved it. The show was fast-paced and less structured than the typical newscast. It allowed me the freedom to improvise and make comments outside of the script. I was in my element. And in the process, the public got to see me in a different light.

Shortly thereafter, the male anchor of *Noticias y Más* left the company for good. This time it was Myrka who needed a new cohost. The producers immediately thought of me, and after careful consideration I accepted the challenge. It was time to move forward and reinvent myself.

In 1994 the show's name was changed to *Primer Impacto,* and it became the first newscast in Hispanic television to be coanchored by two women. Myrka and I had instant chemistry and played off each other perfectly. She was sweet and prudent, while I was irreverent and opinionated. They called us "sugar and spice."

We became household names. People tuned in to hear all the relevant news and to see what new outfits we were wearing. Although short skirts and cleavage might have been a no-no for straight news broadcasts, we were tantalizing, with a winning combination of sexy and serious. Our crossed legs under the clear fiberglass desk became our trademark, and the ratings went through the roof.

It didn't take long for all of us to see that we had captured lightning in a bottle. When all the entertainment magazines began putting *us* on their covers, and following our personal lives like the chapters of a *telenovela,* we knew we had something special. Instead of just reading the news, we became the news.

For years *Primer Impacto* was the most popular show in Hispanic television—ironically, more talked about even than *Noticiero Univision* weekday edition, to which I had originally aspired.

By being flexible and open to every opportunity, I have discovered that often a sidetrack can actually be a shortcut to reaching your goals. And in some cases, it can take you even further, to a place that you never dreamed of.

13

HESITATION IS FOR THE TIMID. AND THE DEAD.

If you want to make it to the top, you need to pay your dues. Especially if you want to *stay* at the top. It is in the process that you learn the skills to survive up there.

When civil unrest erupted in Haiti in September 1991, the Univision news director looked around the newsroom for volunteers.

"Who wants to cover the coup d'état in Haiti?"

Jean-Bertrand Aristide, the first democratically elected

leader of that country, had just been overthrown by the army and there were reports of rampant violence in the streets of the capital, Port-au-Prince. It was an incredibly dangerous situation, but I didn't hesitate. My hand was the first to go up.

Many of the journalists I was working with were seasoned veterans who had done their share of war reporting. They had proven themselves over the years, covering volatile conflicts such as this one. And now it was my turn. I saw it as an opportunity to demonstrate that I was a committed journalist to the core, and I wasn't about to let it pass, even if it meant taking a risk.

Since Haiti was in a state of siege and the airports were closed to commercial flights, my producer, my cameraman, and I flew to Santo Domingo, Dominican Republic—the closest we could get. As we sat having sodas in the hotel lobby figuring out what to do, we met a team of French journalists who had special permission from the Haitian government to land in Port-au-Prince the next day. They had just arrived from Afghanistan, where they had been covering the civil war for the French press. These were rough-and-tumble foreign reporters who took great pride in telling their war stories and musing on the many times they had escaped death. We agreed to partner up to get into Haiti; they had the country's permission to enter and we had the plane. Before the night ended, my team and I half-jokingly scribbled our Last Will and Testaments on the backs of cocktail napkins. We all laughed. But I'd be lying if I said I wasn't scared.

After we landed in Port-au-Prince, I shared a taxi with the French reporters because the car Univision had rented was packed with the driver, the cameraman, the producer, and all the equipment we had brought along. We hadn't driven five minutes when we came upon the first bloodied corpses piled up in the street.

Following the orders of his producer, the French cameraman jumped out of the cab and began filming the carnage. My mind was still adjusting to the scene when a group of very agitated and heavily armed men swarmed the car. One of them stuck his weapon through the open window directly at my temple, his eyes bulging as he railed in Creole.

The world seemed to move in slow motion and yet my mind was racing. All of my senses were enhanced.

I said the first thing that came to mind, the only phrase that I remembered from French 101: *"Je ne comprends pas."* ("I don't understand.")

The man seemed perplexed at my response, both confused and amused.

It was then that I heard someone yelling.

The French producer was screaming at his cameraman in Creole. He seemed to be furious, and as soon as the cameraman approached, he slapped him, chastising him for getting out of the car and filming the scene. The producer acted as if the cameraman was a renegade who had disobeyed his orders, putting our lives at risk. The leader of the Haitian mob lowered his bayonet-tipped rifle and turned around. *Everything is under control,* he seemed to say to his followers. They clearly respected the chain of command when they saw it, so they backed off, including the one holding a gun barrel to my head.

They let us pass and we drove off as the French reporters laughed and laughed about the whole thing. They thought it was hilarious. After all, they had just come back from Afghanistan, where they had perfected their system for getting out of jams like this. When their producer saw that I was still shaken, he tried to calm me down, saying, "Don't worry, they were just pointing their weapons. Worry when you hear them cock their rifles."

My cameraman and I spent the next two weeks dodging bullets during the day, and I, dodging passes at night from a producer who made advances on me in the middle of this chaos. On more than one occasion he tried to grab my feet, insisting that a good massage would help me relax.

The day we were set to leave, I felt relieved and accomplished. The assignment had been a success and I had proven to my colleagues and to my boss that I was a hard-core journalist. I knew I had earned my stripes, reaching a level of credibility that would undoubtedly help my career.

Since we had two hours to kill before our flight, we decided to drive to downtown Port-au-Prince to find a local market where we could buy crafts. We celebrated with our driver the whole way. He was a real character who the first day we met him had handed us a business card that read: translator, bodyguard, tour guide, chauffeur, and voodoo drums teacher. He cranked up the radio, and we beat the drums against the seats and dashboard of the cab as we rumbled through the city.

The music was so loud that we didn't hear the gunshots.

Suddenly, we saw a surge of people running toward us, past our car, fleeing in panic. When we rolled down the windows, we heard gunfire up ahead. It was clear there was work to do. The driver backed up the car and drove onto a side street. We ended up right behind Haitian soldiers firing against a crowd of street demonstrators.

"Let's film it," I said to my cameraman. We got out of the car and moved closer and closer to the Haitian soldiers, who were so focused that they did not even notice us. Until the cameraman got too close.

One of the soldiers slapped a higher-ranking officer on the shoulder and pointed at us, filming them as they fired in the direction of the crowd. They all turned to us at once. He said something in Creole and the soldiers raised their weapons.

Apparently our driver forgot that he was supposed to be our translator and bodyguard and promptly crouched inside the car, hiding under the steering wheel.

It was then that we heard the *clack-clack* of rifles cocking—and the world seemed to slow down, a second lasting a lifetime, as it does in times of danger. *"Worry when you hear them cock their rifles."*

My mind flashed to my first five minutes in Haiti, when the French producer berated his cameraman and saved our skins. I remained cool even as the tension increased, and I borrowed a page from my French counterpart's survival guide.

"Get back in the car!" I yelled at my cameraman, moving quickly toward him.

To make up for the Creole I could not speak, I began pounding on him with my fists. I wanted to communicate disapproval with my gestures. If they could read my body language, see the chain of command at work, perhaps we could get out of this alive.

"What are you doing filming all this? Have you lost your mind?" I screamed, flailing and pointing back at the car, just like I'd seen the French producer do.

My cameraman was puzzled.

"But you told me—" he started, before I cut him off.

"I said get back in car, you idiot!"

Out of the corner of my eye, I could see the Haitian soldiers lowering their rifles and I could almost read their thoughts: *Everything seems under control. We have more important things to worry about. Let this crazy woman deal with him.*

We hustled back to the car, me pushing and berating my cameraman as we rushed, until we were back inside. Our hearts pounded all the way to the airport.

I had learned a valuable lesson: Had I hesitated, I might never have proven myself with this assignment. Had I hesitated, I might never have survived it.

14

RANDOM ACTS OF KINDNESS ARE OFTEN REWARDED WITH A REAL TREAT.

Gloria was left on our doorstep in the middle of the night.

When we discovered her, she was inside a tiny cage, hungry and desperate to escape. Attached to the cage was an anonymous note that read, "She's dumb and no good for the circus. She eats a whole chicken daily. I can't keep her. Her name is Gloria."

My parents were known for rescuing abandoned and

sick animals, and that was probably why someone left us the female ocelot, which looked like a house cat crossed with a leopard. She was malnourished and scared. That night she ate not one but two chickens.

We built a giant enclosure for her in our backyard, and even though she always remained a wild animal, we grew so attached to her that our parents never took us to an animal circus again.

I was eight years old and that experience marked me for life. I became determined to take a stand against animal abuse, and today I make sure that my children do the same. I teach them by example.

One morning I was late driving my children to school when something caught my attention. I saw a scared-looking dog frozen in the middle of passing traffic, its ears down in dismay. It was an old shaggy female and you could tell she was a house pet, not a stray.

I stopped the car and parked diagonally across the road, blocking all traffic.

"Mami, what are you doing? We're going to be late for school," my daughter, Lara, yelled from the backseat, worried.

"My love, there are some things that are more important

than being twenty minutes late to school. We're saving a life," I told them.

I squatted down in the middle of the road, held my hand out, and called the dog forward. She inspected me with a couple of quick sniffs and began to wag her tail. I checked her collar and was relieved to see that it had a tag with the owner's information. I picked her up and put her in the backseat next to my kids, who laughed and petted the old dog while I pulled off the road to dial the number on the tag.

It turned out that the owner lived only a block away. Yet it still took him thirty minutes to meet us and pick up his dog. He shrugged, saying that he had not even noticed that the old dog had run away. I bit my tongue as he loaded the dog into his car. I was sure the poor pooch would be loose again soon, dodging traffic. My kids were late to school that day, but on this occasion it didn't matter. That morning they learned their most important lesson of the day.

I come from a family that strongly believes that instead of being observers, each of us has the responsibility to take an active role in the face of neglect, cruelty, and abuse. I am convinced that if more people felt this way, ours would be a better world. And it doesn't take much. Even the smallest act of kindness triggers a ripple effect that can transform our lives and the lives of others. Just ask my sister, Astrid.

I was driving down a busy freeway in Miami, the Palmetto, in the pouring rain. There was almost no visibility. I could see only as far as the pickup truck in front of me. That's when I caught a glimpse of the cargo in the bed of the truck. A pair of dogs, one large, the other tiny, were kenneled together in a cage, shifting nervously as the unrelenting rain soaked them through and through.

I sped up next to the vehicle, lowered my window, and waved at the pickup's driver.

"Where are you taking those dogs?" I yelled.

"I found them on the street. I'm taking them to the pound," he shouted back over the rumble of the rain and our cars.

"But they're going to kill them there!"

He shrugged his shoulders. "I don't care. I just want them out of my neighborhood," he said.

I motioned for him to pull over onto the shoulder. I took a second to look at the dogs—one large, black and brown, like an Australian shepherd mix, and the other some sort of light brown terrier that could have been the twin of Toto from *The Wizard of Oz.* Then I looked around in my car. It was a days-old white BMW with a light beige interior, too small to fit the kennel. So I jumped out, opened the cage, and put the filthy wet dogs in my backseat. They started jumping everywhere with excitement, as if they knew they had been saved.

Already late for work and soaking wet, I drove them to the office of a veterinarian friend of mine, who updated their shots and helped clean them up. But what to do with them now?

I thought of my sister. She had just moved to a suburb of Miami after a recent and painful divorce. She was living alone and had made the conscious decision to close herself completely to love. Like me, she is an animal lover, so I gave her a call.

Those dogs became her babies and gave her a reason to open her heart. One day they found a way to open the gate and escape to the golf course behind her backyard. The manager of the private golf course found the dogs racing through the greens, and instead of getting mad, he petted them and gave them treats. My sister was moved by his kindness and they became friends.

Eight years later, she still has the dogs and even adopted two more—and she is married to the golf course manager, who brought along his cat.

Sometimes, good deeds come dripping wet with good karma.

15

FORGOING GRUDGES IS NOT JUST IN GOOD TASTE. IT'S GOOD KARMA.

The vice president of the News Department at Univision called me into his office and closed the door.

"What do you know about Janneth Quintero?" he asked.

I had not heard that name in nearly two years. And yet, in a moment, upon hearing her name, I was flooded with some of the worst memories of my journalistic career.

Janneth Quintero was the assignment editor at the news desk of the Univision affiliate in New York where I had started my career in the U.S. Hispanic market. But more than that, she symbolized the period that was professionally the darkest for me. From the day I arrived from Puerto Rico, where I had cut my teeth as an anchor and reporter on a twenty-four-hour news station, Janneth was one of the first people to point out my shortcomings.

I have always had a baby face, a trait that I am now thankful for but which worked against me when I was starting out in the business. Never mind that I had proven myself as a reputable journalist before heading into that job. From the outset, Janneth was one of the first to say I looked too young to be the station's anchor—no one wants to have important news read to them by a child.

Furthermore, she disliked the way I read the news. My Puerto Rican accent was instantly recognizable. We were giving the news to a mélange of Spanish-speaking nationalities in New York and I needed to have a more neutral accent. She was from Colombia, a country that prides itself on having a beautiful, proper Spanish accent. She suggested more than once that I needed classes to improve my diction.

Last but not least, she joined the choir that criticized the handful of outfits that I rotated on air. During a period where the man who had hired me had been replaced and his successor was trying to get me to quit, Janneth's . . . *observations* . . . sank me further into a depression. Those comments chipped away at my self-assurance, and I felt self-conscious on air. The more I became aware, the more I stumbled, and the more insecure and self-conscious I became.

And now my boss was bringing Janneth Quintero's name out of the past. He had an opening for an editor on the national news desk at Univision in Miami. It would be a huge career jump for Janneth, a chance to leave the local market and go network, where she would be working on internationally televised shows.

"I know you worked with her in New York," my boss told me. "So, what do you think? Should I hire her?"

I thought about Janneth. I thought about all the things I had been through. And by that point I knew why Janneth had made my life hell.

The reason her criticism bothered me so much was because she was right.

She was right about my baby face. Right about my accent. Right about my need to wear more glamorous outfits as I read the news to a fashion-conscious New York audience. It was truth that hurt. And it was hard to accept, given everything else I was going through.

But in the months and years after I met her, I worked hard on changing the things she and others criticized me about. I consulted an expert who taught me how to apply my makeup so that I would look more mature and sophisticated. I worked with a speech coach until I achieved a more neutral Spanish accent. And I paid more attention to the clothes I wore on the air. Under the guidance of a professional stylist, I eventually became a regular on the best-dressed lists of several magazines. Even *Vogue en Español* featured me in one of its fashion spreads. Yes, Janneth's criticism gave me an incentive to improve.

I knew my boss valued my opinion, and that a flat-out poor recommendation might have sealed off any advancement for Janneth. At that moment, I could have made the emotional decision to hold Janneth responsible for everything that had gone wrong. All I needed was to say the word.

But if there was one thing I learned from swimming, from sports in general, it is that you may have a talented teammate with whom you do not get along, but when it comes time for competition, you want her on your relay team.

I knew Janneth's work. I knew, despite our personal conflict, that she was a gifted editor with good ideas who was stuck in a bad job. She had outgrown the position years ago and needed a change. She needed someone to give her an opportunity to do bigger and better things.

And that's exactly what I told my boss. He hired her that week.

Janneth came aboard and it was as if she were a new person. She was reenergized in her new job, enthusiastic, bursting with ideas. It wasn't long before we were working on projects together, helping each other's ideas flourish, and I, too, felt rewarded by our relationship.

We shared an activist's mentality, eager to use our journalistic resources to denounce injustices in the world. Together we decided to collaborate on a special series about animal abuse in American and Mexican rodeos. She produced the segments, and soon after, we were honored with a Genesis Award by the Ark Trust Fund, an organization that recognizes members of the media who expose animal cruelty. It was a first for Spanish-language television.

Initially, the network said it could pay for only me to go to Los Angeles and receive the award, but I put my foot down and told them that Janneth deserved the award as much as I did. Either we both went, or neither did.

A year after we gave each other a second chance, Janneth and I were onstage accepting an award together.

The posh cocktail reception thrown by the Ark Trust Fund took place in a sprawling Hollywood Hills mansion overlooking a breathtaking view of the city. It was buzzing with beautiful people who were beautifully dressed. A gallery of sumptuous vegetarian dishes the likes of which I never imagined could be prepared was spread for all of us to enjoy.

The two of us were talking and joking, enjoying the atmosphere, shaking hands with celebrities including actor Pierce Brosnan, who played James Bond at the time. I looked at Janneth Quintero. I had never told her how she had helped make my life hell. And I never told her how right she was in her criticism, either. But I knew then that if I had held a grudge against her, we never would have worked together and achieved this goal that was so important to both of us.

Years later, after I left Univision to start my own show, *Al Rojo Vivo con María Celeste,* she came with me. And we remain good friends and colleagues.

That's why you can never let grudges and resentments rule your decisions. If you do, in your attempt to hurt someone else, the person you stand to hurt the most is yourself.

16

YOUR MIND IS A POWERFUL TOOL. DON'T LET IT WORK AGAINST YOU.

Our minds can make or break us. Your mind can be your best friend or your worst enemy.

I learned that firsthand in September 2001, just days after the 9/11 terror attacks on the World Trade Center and the Pentagon. The Univision newsroom in Miami was busy as can be, and I was working twenty-four/seven covering the aftermath of the tragedy.

Everyone at *Primer Impacto,* the show I was cohosting,

was exhausted from working so many long hours. I had a very bad cold with a fever and nonstop coughing and chills. My colleague Ibis Menéndez, who sat next to me, had the same flulike symptoms and trouble breathing. We figured that we had spent too much time working, our defenses were down, and one of us had given this lousy cough to the other. But even in our mounting exhaustion and illness, we kept each other going. Ibis, who had earned a master's in philosophy in the Soviet Union, is smart and witty, and she helped make the long hours bearable.

And then we saw a bizarre piece of news on the wires. A sixty-three-year-old photo editor at the *Sun* tabloid in Florida had died after inhaling anthrax. Just a few days before, a mysterious white powder had puffed into the air as he opened a letter addressed to actress Jennifer Lopez, sent care of the *Sun*. It was the anthrax bacteria in its most lethal form.

We reported the strange incident on our show that afternoon, because this man was the first person in the United States to die from this rare disease in twenty-five years.

Then the other letters came.

One after another, new cases of anthrax exposure were being reported across the country—in network newsrooms, post offices, and congressional offices. The first five letters containing anthrax spores had been mailed on September 18 to the New York headquarters of ABC News, CBS News, NBC News, and the *New York Post,* and to the *National Enquirer* in Florida. Days later, two more letters were mailed to congressmen in Washington, D.C.

It was clearly a bioterror attack. The public was in a panic, and finding a small amount of white powder was enough to mobilize hazardous materials teams and cause the evacuation of whole buildings. We, the media, went into a frenzy trying to catch up with all the reports of possible anthrax exposure around the country, which often turned out to be false alarms. The collective fear was so intense that even a few grains of baking soda or laundry detergent seemed menacing.

Ibis and I neglected sleep, and as the days went on, we noticed that our symptoms had worsened.

Then we received a memo informing us that due to the possible wave of terror attacks, absolutely no letters or packages would be delivered to the newsroom until further notice. And a latent memory washed over Ibis and me like ice water.

A few days earlier, I had received a very odd package at the office. It was a cardboard box sealed tightly with so much brown tape that I had to ask Ibis to help me open it.

When Ibis opened it, a cloud of dust hit her directly in the face and then it hit me. The box contained only a letter that didn't make much sense, and a bunch of crumbled newspapers. *Dusty* newspapers.

We didn't think much of it at the time. "It must be from some crazy fan," she said. And so we threw the box in the trash and didn't give it another thought.

Until we saw that memo and it all made sense: *My God, we have anthrax!*

Our minds started racing. The more we thought about it, the more paranoid we became, and the worse our cold symptoms seemed to get. Just like the anthrax victims, we had sore throats, muscle pain, and fever, and we were struggling to breathe. Could it be possible?

We had no choice but to tell our news director. She listened and after a long, pregnant pause called the public relations department of a well-known Miami hospital and spoke to a contact. This had to be kept secret from the media until we knew for sure.

Ibis and I rushed to the hospital and were taken to an isolated wing where the doctors and nurses wore face masks and approached us carefully. They ran a battery of tests and finally showed us X-rays of our lungs. Ibis was diagnosed with full-blown pneumonia, and I with severe bronchitis, borderline pneumonia, all symptoms consistent with anthrax exposure.

We were told that samples of our blood were being rushed to a specialized out-of-state lab where they would be tested for exposure to the deadly bacteria and that the results would be back within three days. At that time, they would have definite answers.

In the meantime, doctors started us on a heavy regimen of the antibiotic ciprofloxacin, Cipro, which was being given to all the anthrax victims and then, to our surprise, they sent us home. They probably figured that it was highly unlikely we had anthrax, since so much time had elapsed from the day we had opened the mysterious dusty package. Besides, we'd been sick for a while, with no sign of suffering from shock, which afflicts anthrax victims within days of exposure.

Even though it didn't add up, we wouldn't listen. Our minds had taken us beyond reason, and all we could think of was that we had anthrax.

We spent the next seventy-two hours talking to each other on the phone in a state of controlled panic, overanalyzing every symptom.

Manny Arvesú, my second husband, thought I was being overly dramatic. "You both went almost two weeks with untreated bronchitis and pneumonia. . . . If it were anthrax, wouldn't you be dead by now?" he asked me more than once. "I think you have been spending way too much time in the newsroom and it's getting to you."

I was furious at him for his insensitivity. Here I was dying, and my husband didn't seem to care!

Finally, we received the results: negative for anthrax.

Yes, we felt an incredible sense of relief. We were going to live! But we would have to live with the embarrassment of knowing that we had alarmed our families, our coworkers, and everyone at the hospital with our anthrax paranoia.

We were two intelligent women feeling very stupid. We had let our fears take over, allowing our all-powerful minds to play a trick on us.

By the end of the anthrax attacks, twenty-two people had been infected and five had died. Almost seven years later, authorities finally named a suspect. It turned out to be an army bio-defense scientist who committed suicide upon learning that he would be charged and tried for the 2001 attacks.

By the time it was all over, I had learned a big lesson: Never underestimate the power of suggestion. The mind is our most powerful weapon. We can let it run wild with fear and doubt, or we can train it to focus on facts, not fiction. Our thoughts can shape our reality. And in some instances, distort it.

17

YOU HAVE ONLY ONE LIFE TO LIVE. LIVE IT A LITTLE DANGEROUSLY.

A dear friend of mine who loves the ocean always says, "When sailing, don't try to escape the rough seas, or you will never become a skillful sailor." I believe the same applies to life.

Instead of running away from our fears, we should conquer them. Otherwise, we will miss incredible opportunities to acquire knowledge and live life to the fullest.

I was five months pregnant with my son Julian when I

went to Africa for the first time. It was a trip that my second husband, Manny, and I had been planning for more than a year, along with my dear friends Raúl and Mily de Molina, who are seasoned world travelers. When the time came, we decided to go ahead with the trip, in spite of my pregnancy. I remember that in the days before our departure, my mother would call me on a daily basis to try to dissuade me from going.

"Mari, you're crazy to go there so far along in your pregnancy. What if you get malaria?" she would say over and over.

"Mami, I'm not going to stop living out of fear of what may or may not happen," I would tell her. "I'm going to be very careful, but I'm still going!"

Little did we know that the real danger awaiting me was not a tiny mosquito carrying malaria, but an enormous elephant.

From the moment we arrived at the eco-friendly lodge of Sandibe, Botswana, we were told "beware of elephants." At the time, there was an overpopulation of elephants in that part of Africa, so the government was allowing them to be hunted. As you might expect, elephants were very wary of humans and acted aggressively if you got too close.

But the larger problem was Raúl. Although he had been

working as a television host for many years, he still remembered his days as a freelance photographer for *Time* magazine. Photography is his passion and he thrives on getting up close and personal with wild animals—elephants included.

The afternoon of our first safari, he loaded the jeep with all of his camera equipment, and I loaded my bag with every type of insect repellent available. My concern was still malaria, so I also wore clothes that covered as much skin as possible and prayed that I wouldn't get bitten.

Once on the road, we came across many elephants, and every time Raúl would ask our ranger to drive in closer to them. Often the animals would make loud warning noises to shoo us away. But Raúl would ignore them, insisting we stay put while he clicked away. It made the elephants nervous.

"Why did you bring all those lenses to take pictures from a distance if you were going to be in their faces?" I teased.

"I didn't come all the way out here to see them from afar," he responded. "For that, I could have stayed at home and watched them on the Discovery Channel."

Mind you, to him, "afar" meant fifteen feet, versus five.

The ranger got a kick out of our arguments. Both he and a tracker, a native expert in finding the animals who was perched on a seat in front of the vehicle, would tell us there was nothing to worry about unless the elephant started scratching the ground, which hadn't happened—yet.

And so we went on our daily safaris until it was almost time to return home. On our last morning drive, we went looking for leopards along a path of fallen trees and bushes. I was a bit uneasy because the terrain made it difficult to see what lay ahead, and the last thing we wanted was to startle an elephant. Which is exactly what happened. We turned a curve and right in front of us was a bull elephant, only a few feet away. Apparently, there was a herd passing by and we had unsuspectingly gotten ourselves in the middle of it. We had dangerously invaded their territory and the male elephant reacted exactly the way we were afraid he would.

He started scraping the ground with his giant foot.

In a split second, we saw the tracker do a somersault from his seat and land in the front passenger's seat, next to the ranger.

As the elephant spat a cloud of dust at us with his trunk and began charging toward our jeep, the ranger shifted the vehicle into reverse and started speeding frantically in the opposite direction. Two or three seconds into the chase, when it was obvious that we were going to be outrun and there was no way to escape, the most amazing thing happened. A deer ran between the jeep and the charging elephant, stopping the behemoth in its tracks. For an instant, the elephant was frazzled, and to our surprise—and relief—he chased the deer instead.

By the time we caught our breath, we realized we had crashed against some thorny tree. Everyone in the backseat was covered in thorns. But no one spoke a word.

Raúl finally broke the silence to ask Manny, who had been filming our excursion, if he had gotten that on tape. Indeed, he had recorded the entire episode. And the following week, Raúl ran the video on his television show.

There's no doubt this story would not have had a happy ending if not for the ranger's quick reflexes and the unsuspecting deer.

Aside from leaving us with a great story, that close call also left me with an important lesson: Danger awaits around every corner, whether it is a furious elephant in the African savannah or a slip and fall in your living room. Our days on this magnificent planet are numbered. Yet the beauty and the horror of it is that we don't know when our last call will be. So we have to enjoy life to the fullest.

In spite of that encounter with the elephant, I have since returned to visit Kenya, South Africa, and Tanzania. I'm glad

I didn't allow that incident to traumatize me to the point of not wanting to return to that magical continent. I would not have been able to kiss a giraffe in a Nairobi sanctuary or see a hippo nursing her calf in a pond in Tanzania or witness a crocodile devouring an old wildebeest struggling for life in the Serengeti.

Instead of being afraid, we have to be daring in the face of our mortality. And we have to choose: Do we wait for the inevitable as observers, or do we play an active role in our lives? It is up to us. As for me, I'd rather risk being devoured by a tiger or slipping down a cliff while climbing a volcano.

I choose to be an active player rather than an observer.

I choose to live. And I hope my children do the same. More than anything, I dream of returning to Africa with my son Julian by my side.

18

LISTEN TO YOUR SIXTH SENSE.

Before we can form words, before we can smile or frown, before we can even look our parents in the eyes, we can communicate.

Our biology, developed over millions of years of evolution, has equipped us with a sixth sense that alerts us to danger. It cannot be explained by logic or reason, and being attuned to it is key to survival.

I know this now.

My son Julian was asking for help.

He was born prematurely at just thirty weeks, weighing a little more than five pounds. He needed all of my attention and then some. He had to be fed every hour, on the hour, and the physical toll became too much. So I hired a kind woman to help me with him and the daily chores. She came highly recommended and her disposition told me she was a perfect choice. She worked hard, was always attentive to his cries, was at his beck and call. Her name was Angela and she was, as I often told her, my angel. Whenever I left him with her in the morning, she cradled him lovingly in her arms. When I returned from errands, they would be in the same position, with Julian suckling a bottle hungrily and our black chow chow, Chula, sitting at their feet. The image was picture perfect, yet I couldn't explain the anxious feelings I was having when I was away—or why my baby was so sick.

At first we thought it was the formula that was making Julian, my firstborn, so ill. But no matter what formula we put him on, he responded day after day with vomiting fits. It didn't seem to be upset stomach or reflux or general crankiness. At six weeks old, he couldn't keep his food down.

I know now that it was his way of telling me that something was very wrong.

When Julian was eight weeks old, my husband, Manny,

finally convinced me to get out of the house to see our first movie together in months.

We sat in the theater and as he watched the film, my mind wandered to the churning in my stomach. To this day, I do not remember what movie we watched. What I remember is the urging from a voice within, a silent primal scream, to run home from the movie theater.

"Let's go back," I said in the middle of the film.

"What? Mari, you're being overprotective. Don't be paranoid," he told me, trying to calm me.

We sat in the dark for the rest of whatever film that was, and I tried to keep from jumping out of my skin. My intuition that something was wrong was stronger than a feeling. It was certainty.

The car had barely stopped in the driveway when I got out, rushed into the house, and found Julian . . . perfectly safe in Angela's arms, asleep, nursing from his bottle.

Maybe Manny's right, I thought. *I shouldn't worry so much*. . . . Maybe the videos of caregivers abusing children that we so often featured on our show were getting to me. Still, every time I left the house without Julian, the voice inside my head was no less subdued. I decided to hire a company to install a hidden camera in my bedroom, overlooking the baby's crib. The installer had one piece of advice: Before leaving the nanny home alone, I should tell her that I would be gone the whole day and not to expect me back until late. "That way," he said, "she will lower her guard and show her true colors." More than ever, the rational part of me felt like a hysterical mother.

I tried the camera out on a Friday. I kissed Julian and placed him in his crib early in the morning. I told Angela, my angel, that his milk was in the refrigerator and reminded her that his next feeding was in half an hour. I would be gone all day, I told her, and would not be back until about four in the afternoon. I left them just like that, the baby kicking in his crib, Angela smiling.

I fought my squirming insides throughout the morning, running errands to distract myself. But as four p.m. approached, I could no longer fight the screaming inside me to come home. When I unlocked the door, I found the same familiar scene: Angela gently rocking my baby, cooing to him like a grandmother as he drank from his bottle, our black dog wagging her tail nearby.

When my husband returned from work, I sent Angela home for the weekend so that we could watch the tape in private. As Manny started to cue it up, I felt such an overwhelming anxiety that I had to leave the room before the video started.

"I can't watch," I told him.

Deep down, I knew the tape held something terrible.

Manny watched it as I waited in the adjacent living room. At one point I thought I could hear a baby crying. Tears welled in my own eyes. After what seemed like an eternity, Manny trudged out of the room, white as a sheet, looking as if he was on the verge of being physically ill.

"It's really bad," he said.

What I would see on the tape proved my instincts right.

The second I walk out the door, Chula runs and sits protectively under the crib. Thirty minutes later, when it's time for Julian's bottle, he starts to squirm and call out. Then he cries. And cries. He cries harder, desperately, wailing for his milk. Finally Angela approaches the crib, leans over, and punches my baby with her fist.

"Enough!" she yells with a blow that sends a shock wave through Julian's nine-pound body.

There is a second of silence. Then my baby begins to howl with interminable shrieks.

Julian cries himself to sleep, waking up hungry, and then falling asleep again, exhausted. Meanwhile, Angela rifles through my drawers while talking to her friends on the phone, commenting on what a brat my weeks-old infant is.

Chula remained by the crib, as if, in some way, she were trying to guard the baby from his attacker. When the dog's ears perk up and she dashes off barking, Angela hurries offscreen, returns with a bottle, and starts feeding Julian on the rocking chair. I hear a door open and my voice announcing that I'm home.

The force of the punch was so intense that the doctor who saw the tape at Miami Children's Hospital immediately performed a full body scan. Julian's own pediatrician wept at the sight of the video. But babies are resilient. He was not injured in that attack or the others that Angela later confessed to in front of police. He was fine even after the time she grabbed him by the ankles and dangled him upside down, shaking him, as she acknowledged. She insisted that she had done nothing wrong, that she took care of him as if he were her own, even giving him a home remedy made with star anise when he was colicky. *Star anise,* which can cause seizures and neurological damage. And that's what she *admitted* to. I can only guess what her conscience would not let her vocalize.

And because Julian suffered no injuries, Angela didn't receive jail time. She was only ordered to attend anger management classes and to perform community service. For all I know, she is still free on the streets of Miami. The only person who paid any price for the attack was Julian, and we who were left with the guilt and emotional bruising.

The amazing thing was the change we immediately saw in Julian. Within days of Angela being arrested, he stopped throwing up his milk and quickly put on weight. He became one of those happy, gurgling babies who rarely spit up or cried.

I realized that all his previous health problems were a reaction to the mistreatment and abuse he was being subjected to. "Before babies can talk, they communicate with their bodies," the pediatrician explained.

According to the surveillance experts, when clients rent a hidden camera suspecting that their children are being abused, seven times out of ten they are correct.

If I knew then what I know now, I would have not struggled with my sixth sense. I would not have waited for a camera to confirm what my instincts were telling me all along.

Forget reason. When your intuition says something is wrong, pay attention. It will never fail you.

19

SOMETIMES LOVE FINDS YOU. OTHER TIMES, YOU WILL FIND IT IN HIDDEN PLACES.

Lights from Red Square glimmered through my hotel room window as I packed my bags to leave Moscow.

I stopped for a moment to stand at the window and look down at the snow-covered square. A feeling so thorough washed over me, a nostalgia, a longing, like a great, impending adventure—something much bigger than the assignment that brought me here from Channel 24 in Puerto Rico. I would see this place again, would return here one day—I knew it—and goose bumps raised the hair on the back of my neck.

What could evoke such an emotion?

I interpreted it as romantic love. Although I was married to Guillermo at the time, I could not shake the feeling that this place, this country, would await me again with a great love, a life-changing experience. I felt it in my bones.

When Manny, my second husband, and I decided to adopt a child, I made my intentions very clear.

"We're not going shopping," I told him.

The adoption agency said they would send us photos of children via the Internet. They would send one at a time, and if we didn't get the right feeling about a child, we could ask them to send another. But I had made up my mind before the first photo popped up on my computer at work.

"The first one we see, we're going to take," I told Manny. "Whoever it is, it's meant to be."

When I was a little girl, I vowed to adopt a child. The thought of an infant—a little boy, a little girl—set adrift by apathy or circumstance left an empty place in my heart. The desire to adopt stayed with me for years: after my first marriage;

after meeting Manny; after my oldest, my son Julian, was born. The feeling stayed with me, always.

And then one day I introduced a story on television about a particular orphanage in Central America run by nuns for the children of an indigenous people. I watched the segment live for the first time, and when it ended, I composed myself enough to go to commercial. But I knew something had reawakened in me. And I was ready to fulfill my childhood promise.

Manny and I spent the next few months looking to adopt, even as I became pregnant with my daughter, Lara. We encountered many challenges in Latin America, the Caribbean, and Asia. Our best hope came from an orphanage in a little town called Stupino, two hours from Moscow. They requested pictures of us so they could try to match us with a child who looked like us, so that as he grew he would feel more connected, they said. Some of my friends asked whether we wouldn't feel more comfortable with a child from a Latin American country. But we didn't care what country he came from. A child in need has no nationality.

The boy in the first picture I opened on my computer had a vacant stare. His cheeks were gaunt. And by just looking at him lying in his threadbare pink pajamas, I could tell his body was weak. Malnourished. And yet I knew he was the one.

His name was Vadim. He was thirteen months old.

Manny and I flew halfway around the world to Moscow, me carrying a belly five months pregnant with a child we had just learned would be a girl. We arrived late and tired, and spent the night in a hotel where I fell into a deep sleep, exhausted, dreaming of my little boy.

The next morning, we drove for two hours under an overcast sky until we reached Stupino, the small town where Vadim lived. We bought him a toy at a small store before heading to the orphanage, which was just a short drive away.

The building was humble, squat, paint peeling from the walls. But rows of flowers adorned the garden. A sign above the door to the orphanage read simply, "Little Ray of Sunlight."

We stepped inside and I was stopped at the door by an odor that resembled burned fish. It was dark, the walls dreary, not painted in years. One staffer led us down the hall and opened the door to a large, open room where the wails and gurgles of about forty babies resonated. We were led to a small visitor's area, where a baby waited in a crib. He was Baby Number Six—so said the number written on his pajamas and bedsheet. Vadim.

Although Vadim was at an age where he should be near walking, he was barely able to sit, and even then, not for very long. With one nurse in charge of about twenty children, the little orphans often spent their days on their backs, their abdominal muscles underdeveloped. I asked to hold him. His clothes, too large, were filthy and smelled of humidity.

"Carry him gently as to not scare him," my husband was told when it was his turn. "He's not used to seeing men."

We could hear the wails and moans of other children as I looked into the deep, dark eyes of my baby boy.

"Can we take him outside," I asked a caretaker, "to have a little time alone with him?"

It was a strange request, they said, and they wondered how he would react. "Why?" I asked. After his birth, Vadim was brought to the orphanage by night.

"He has never seen the light of day," they said.

I barely slept that night.

After spending the afternoon with Vadim, images of him kept flashing in my mind as I tried to rest. He never seemed to look us in the eye. Instead, he looked far off, lost. I remembered how my son Julian was already walking at thirteen months. Vadim could hardly sit or crawl. I could not deny that this little baby had deep, severe issues. And I worried how I would be able to be the mother he needed.

I woke Manny up and shared my fears with him.

Together, we called Julian's pediatrician back home, where it was morning. We talked for a long time about all the special care Vadim would likely need. I was committed to the little boy with the deep, dark eyes from the second I saw him, and I wanted to make sure he would have a strong support system. Our pediatrician promised that he would help us every step of the way and added something that I will never forget: "Love is the best medicine."

I lay in bed and prayed, prayed that this would be a positive step for all of us. The next two months would seem like a lifetime, I thought, as we waited the mandatory period before taking Vadim home. It was meant as a cooling-off period, to make sure we were certain of our decision. But I was ready to take him right then and there.

When my son turned five years old, I gave him a wooden music box that I had bought in Moscow the afternoon I met him. It is a replica of the famous St. Basil's Cathedral in Red Square.

"What is it, Mamá?" he asked.

"It's a little piece of Russia that I've been keeping for you." I turned the key and "Lara's Theme" from the movie *Doctor Zhivago* began emanating from the player. My son smiled with a twinkle in his eyes and my heart sang. I've always loved that movie. It's why I named my daughter Lara, after the protagonist's love interest. Lara was born two months after Vadim came home with us and became Adrian Vadim.

The first few months were difficult for all of us, but mostly for Adrian. Since no one ever spoke to him at the orphanage, he never learned to make the cooing sounds other children his age make as a preamble to speaking. He knew only how to grunt and had to undergo months of speech therapy to learn how to talk. He needed physical therapy to strengthen his abdominal muscles, so he could sit up straight, crawl, and eventually walk. And he needed occupational therapy to learn how to relate to people, to connect with his family and peers.

Because of the lack of human contact, his nervous system was stunted. Being caressed was so overwhelming a sensation that it was like torture to him; the touch of even a feather was excruciating. On doctor's orders, we had to brush his entire body firmly with a brush every two hours for two months to help stimulate the development of his sensory nerves.

And no thanks to the thick gruel they'd fed him at the orphanage, he had a retarded digestive tract that made him scream in agony whenever he had a bowel movement.

Even the events that we assumed would be routine were complicated. He was terrified of bath time. At the beginning, we would put him in the bathtub and he would scream in terror. Since babies were bathed in an assembly-line style at the orphanage, without a loving mother to check the temperature, he probably was washed with water that was either freezing cold or so hot that it burned his skin. It wasn't until we had him take baths with Julian that he learned there was nothing to fear.

It took weeks for him to recover from a diaper rash so severe that it eroded his skin in parts, leaving a quarter-inch indentation on his soft little bottom. Back in Stupino, he often went an entire day with a soiled diaper.

More than anything, Adrian received the therapy that only love could provide. He learned to look us in the eye, to hug us, to show empathy. He learned to love.

Now he asks for "our" time, to sit with me and tell me all about the love trials a nine-year-old faces at school. The one girl whose picture he keeps under his pillow. The one with whom he shares his snacks and to whom he gives little gifts, and the other, who won't return his affection.

"If she's too dumb to notice how special you are, then she doesn't deserve your time," I tell him.

"Mamá," he once replied sharply, "please don't ever speak that way again about the woman I love."

He has blossomed before my eyes into a person of strong emotions and convictions with an incredible capacity to love. I thought I was doing something amazing for him, and it is he who has done something amazing for me.

I remember the time he asked me how come Julian and Lara had come out of my belly and he hadn't.

"Because you were born in my heart," I told him. "You're so special that we went to the other side of the world just to find you."

To this day he keeps the music box in a special place in his room. Sometimes he takes it out and looks at it intensely, taking in every detail and every color. As I see his tiny hand holding it I think of how much he's overcome, and memories from my first time in Moscow, years before, wash over me. St. Basil's Cathedral. Red Square. My great love.

"What is this building, Mamá?" he asked me once.

"That is your castle, Adrian Vadim." I kissed his forehead. "And you are my prince."

A prince who brought sunshine into our lives even before he had seen the sun.

20

YOUR NAME IS YOUR MOST PRIZED POSSESSION.

No matter what we do on this earth, the most important legacy we will pass on to our children is our name. It can be a source of either pride or shame, and it's up to us to decide how we will be remembered. I learned this lesson from a young woman I came to know better in death than in life.

She was born Selena Quintanilla. She was a singer who became a star—the Queen of Tex-Mex music, they called her—but that was not her dream. She had always wanted to design clothes. Yet it was her powerful satin voice that brought the Mexican-American star her unimaginable fame. She was, in a word, just "Selena"—a single name that said it all to the world. I met her briefly when she was rising, burning white-hot the way you expect from a star gone supernova, but it was after her death that I learned more of her legacy.

Her death would be as sudden as her precipitous rise. She was murdered by her trusted assistant, Yolanda Saldívar, and the coverage of her killer's trial would become another chapter in the singer's life. I lived with Selena's story for months, covering Saldívar's trial, digging through thousands of court documents, analyzing Selena's life. After a while, it seemed my days began and ended with the haunting image of Selena's iridescent smile burned into my mind.

When I was approached about writing a book about Selena, it seemed like the appropriate way to channel those feelings. But it was a formidable challenge. I had recently remarried and was working full-time as a cohost of a television show. My hands were full. Besides, I had never written a book before and could type with only two fingers. Then I remembered what my father told me during my swimming days: "Don't stick your toe in the pool, Mari. Just jump in." And so I did.

With the four trophies I won in a 1968 national swimming competition in Ohio, where I earned the nickname Little Meteor. After I became a Central American champion, I went to the United States looking for new challenges.

My wedding day with Guillermo Ramis in San Juan, Puerto Rico, October 12, 1984.

This was my Channel 24 press photo. I was a news anchor and reporter at the station when it launched in Puerto Rico in 1987.

Reporting in the middle of a snowstorm from Moscow's Red Square in December 1987. My special about life in the Soviet Union made history in Puerto Rico.

With the Kremlin in the background, I was covering the new period of reform and openness in the Soviet Union. After that report, my journalistic career took off like a rocket.

Shaking hands with the Reverend Jesse Jackson the night I received the Journalist of the Year award in Puerto Rico in 1988. After the ceremony, I landed an exclusive interview with him that made headlines.

With Myrka Dellanos on the set of Univision's *Primer Impacto* in 1994, shortly after it became the first news show on Spanish-language television to be hosted by two women. Our "sugar and spice" combination was a winner!

With Janneth Quintero in Hollywood in 1995 right after radio personality Casey Kasem handed us the Genesis Award for denouncing animal abuse in American and Mexican rodeos.

My father walked me to the altar the day I married Manny Arvesu in Coconut Grove, Florida, on January 27, 1996.

With Raúl and Milly Demolina and my then husband Manny on a safari along the Okavongo Delta in Botswana, Africa, in September 1997. This picture was taken when I was five months pregnant, only minutes before we were almost trampled by an elephant.

With Manny and the kids only hours after Lara was born via C-section in a Miami hospital on January 10, 2001.

This picture marked a turning point in my career. It was taken on April 10, 2002, the day that Telemundo and NBC announced that I had joined the company as the host and managing editor of *Al Rojo Vivo con María Celeste,* and that I would be collaborating on NBC shows such as *Dateline* and the *Today* show. I'm with (left) Andy Lack, president of NBC, and Jim McNamara, president of Telemundo.

Interviewing Ricky Martin in Miami for *Al Rojo Vivo con María Celeste,* November 17, 2003.

With Emilio and Gloria Estefan and their bulldog puppies at their Star Island home in Miami in 2004.

With actor Mel Gibson in Los Angeles, February 28, 2005.

At my brother Jose Enrique's wedding in Puerto Rico on March 5, 2005. From left to right: my sister Patricia with her son, Noah; my stepmother, Luissette; my brother Gabriel; my father; the groom; myself; my sister Astrid. In the front row are my children, Julian, Adrian, and Lara.

I signed the papers to divorce Manny the same day I received an Emmy in San Antonio, Texas, in June 2005.

This picture was taken in Rockefeller Plaza in New York the first time I cohosted NBC's *Today* show. *The New York Times* published it along with an article about my crossover, "Breaking the Sound Barrier," on July 23, 2006.

With Matt Lauer and Campbell Brown, on that same day in Rockefeller Plaza.

With Anne Curry and Al Roker, minutes after we finished taping the *Today* show.

My billboard in New York's Times Square in May 2006.

Celebrating the fifth anniversary of my Telemundo show, *Al Rojo Vivo con María Celeste,* on April 3, 2007. I'm with (left) Jorge Hidalgo, senior executive vice president of News and Sports, and Don Browne, the president of Telemundo. I wore a bright yellow dress to celebrate that the sun always shines in Telemundo.

With my beautiful daughter, Lara, in Miami in 2007.
(Omar Cruz)

With my children, Lara, Adrian, and Julian, in Miami, May 2007.
(Omar Cruz)

Getting up close and personal with gray whales in Baja California, Mexico, in 2008 was an unforgettable experience.

With Raúl Mateu, my agent from the William Morris Agency, at a party given at the Museum of Modern Art in New York, May 2008.

In the following months, I learned a lot more about the young woman who would not see her twenty-fourth birthday, who recorded her first album at age twelve, who reached Beatles status in much of Latin America, who became a Grammy winner, who secretly dreamed of being an international fashion designer. I worked sixteen-hour days interviewing and reinterviewing witnesses, lawyers, and family members and friends of both Selena and her murderer. I was the first reporter to speak to Yolanda Saldívar in prison, where she was serving a life sentence. In every way, I was touched by Selena's story.

When my book *Selena's Secret* came out, I was pleased that it captured the essence of her final days and that it honored her memory. But Selena's father objected.

Abraham Quintanilla had just produced an upcoming movie about her life, and he was furious because my book contradicted much of what the film portrayed. He threatened to sue me and called my bosses at Univision to complain. He put so much pressure on *Latina* magazine that the publication backed out of printing excerpts of the book.

And he didn't stop there. He accused me of trying to profit from Selena's death. It was a delicate situation because as much as I wanted to defend myself, I knew it wasn't right to confront a grieving father. So I did what I thought was right. In Selena's name, I pledged that all the proceeds from the sale of my book would go to scholarships for low-income aspiring fashion designers. For me, money was not as important as protecting my name and reputation.

Then one day, at the grocery store, I came across an issue of *Time* magazine that featured a cover story about the media frenzy and big business surrounding Selena's death. I immediately bought it and ran home to read it. Imagine my shock when I discovered my own name among the so-called vultures who were profiting from her untimely demise.

> Selena is the latest, largest artifact in the kind of postmortem career maintenance that not only honors but also profits from a slain celebrity. . . . Scavengers are also circling. E! the Entertainment Channel aired a reenactment of Saldívar's trial and plans to rebroadcast it soon. And in *Selena's Secret,* the newest of at least half a dozen unsanctioned bio books about the star, author and Univision hostess María Celeste Arrarás

> coyly hints that Selena kept a secret diary and was planning to torpedo her career . . .

I was stunned. I read the paragraph over and over, feeling both hurt and angry. Didn't they know I had donated the proceeds? A journalist has no commodity greater than his or her reputation. And I felt I had been stripped of mine by a publication that had not even bothered to call me to get my side of the story. I felt a knot in my stomach and felt compelled to call *Time* the second I finished reading the article. I thought I was having a heart attack.

When I asked to speak with the writer of the story or an editor, I was bounced around for several minutes until they eventually blew me off. My mind swirled with scenarios of what the public would think. I thought about my show and my name, which I had worked so hard to build and protect. Now this article threatened to tear it all down with a false association.

I realized what I had to do. I had to fight to clear my name.

I hired an attorney and sued *Time,* demanding a retraction.

On April 6, 1998, in the tiniest of print in the Letters to the Editor section, *Time* ran the following under "Clarification":

> In our article "Viva Selena!" [Cinema, March 24, 1997], we referred to a book called *Selena's Secret* by Univision anchorwoman María Celeste Arrarás. The book reports the results of an investigation into Selena's murder. Although in the article *Time* characterized Ms. Arrarás as one of the "scavengers . . . circling" after Selena's death, we were unaware at the time that Ms. Arrarás had pledged to donate all profits from her book to charity. We apologize for any misunderstanding.

I read and reread that note to myself and have kept a copy framed in my office ever since. It wasn't a front-page retraction, but it was enough for me to know that my name—and by association my children's names—will remain clear. Furthermore, *Selena's Secret* became one of the best-selling nonfiction books in Spanish, and people all over the world learned the revealing story behind her tragic death.

The note is a reminder that your name is built upon every decision you ever make. And when it comes to defending it, you must be relentless. After all, your name is a legacy that lives on after you've gone to the grave.

So what's in a name?

Everything.

21

YOUR WORD IS YOUR CONTRACT. BREAK IT AND RISK LOSING YOUR SOUL.

Loyalty shouldn't have a price, not even if it is a six-figure number, because when we betray someone's trust we lose something that cannot be replaced: our self-respect.

I met my agent, Raúl Mateu, early in my career, when he lived in New York. This was way before he became a hot-shot executive at the prestigious William Morris Agency and moved to Miami to become the head of its Hispanic talent division.

From the very beginning we both had big dreams and a commitment to reach them together. We had nothing to lose and a lot to gain, and in the process we became friends.

That's why he was the first person I reached out to when I became disenchanted with my job as cohost of one of the highest-rated shows on Univision.

In 2000, after coanchoring *Primer Impacto* for several years, I felt that the show needed to evolve, and I wanted to be an active participant in its transformation. On a personal level, I was also yearning for new challenges. I wanted to explore new possibilities in addition to *Primer Impacto.* Yet both options seemed out of reach.

On a daily basis, I had to accept the editorial decisions of producers with little or no experience, many of them second-generation Hispanics born and raised in Miami who spoke limited Spanish and could not relate to most of our viewers in the rest of the country and in Latin America. They were clueless about the realities of our very important Mexican viewers, who composed the majority of our audience. The border was as alien to them as Mars.

Having worked in Puerto Rico, New York, Los Angeles, and Miami, I had firsthand knowledge of what the audiences in the different markets expected of a network newsmagazine such as ours. It was clear to me that the show often lacked vision and substance and that we had to make changes if we wanted to stay on top. I was eager to participate in the editorial decision-making process of the program. Yet this was often an uphill battle.

One day I wanted the producer du jour to include a story about an upcoming strike by the United Farm Workers union, founded years before by civil rights champion Cesar Chavez. Only after I spent twenty minutes explaining to her the legacy of Chavez did she grudgingly agree to eliminate a silly story about Beanie Baby Mania to make time.

In the middle of my frustration, I would vent to Raúl Mateu. We both agreed that my next contract had to include a provision granting me editorial say in the show. This was a deal breaker.

I was also pursuing new creative venues.

Every Tuesday night I would meet with Mario Rodriguez, the vice president of programming for the network, who wanted to develop a television mini-series based on my book *Selena's Secret*. I was very excited about this project and enjoyed working with such a brilliant and supportive professional.

In February 2001, Mario asked the business affairs

department of the network to proceed with the purchase of the screenplay adaptation rights to *Selena's Secret*.

It was only two months before the network's yearly programming presentation to the advertising agencies, and they needed to own the rights before they could officially announce that they were launching the mini-series. Time was of the essence.

But when Raúl called to follow up, the head of business affairs explained that there would be no deal unless I agreed to extend my employment contract and include the rights to the book as part of the package.

Initially I was against the idea because you have more leverage to negotiate as your contract gets closer to its expiration date, and mine still had several months to go. But ultimately, at the insistence of Univision and driven by my enthusiasm for the Selena project, I accepted.

So I waited for Univision's contract offer. And I waited.

In May, two weeks before the network's presentation in New York, we called the business affairs department and were told that they hadn't had time to crunch the numbers in order to figure out what kind of a raise they could offer me. They said they couldn't get to it until after the network's programming presentation.

I felt disheartened and taken for granted. And hours later, I felt outraged when I found out that the company was planning to go ahead with the Selena mini-series presentation, and that for lack of an agreement it wasn't going to mention the book or my name.

Raúl and I decided to fight back. We sent a letter warning the company to cease and desist from its intention to announce the Selena project or there would be legal consequences. We also gave them an ultimatum: Unless we all came to an agreement immediately, the rights to *Selena's Secret* would no longer be available. It was a bold move.

The network attorneys fired back with another letter putting me on notice that if I sold the rights of the book to a third party I would be in breach of my employment agreement at Univision.

It was a standoff.

The next day, I got a call from the president of Univision, Ray Rodriguez, who happens to be a personal friend.

His tone was conciliatory. He didn't want the situation to continue escalating.

"Mari, it's up to you whether we make the announcement or not. Either way, we renegotiate your entire contract later in the summer. I suggest that you go along with us making the announcement and negotiating your contract later. I promise that everything will work out," he said sweetly. I was about to accept his suggestion about going along with the announcement when he made a comment that I interpreted as condescending.

"I understand that you have been getting bad advice," he said.

I knew full well that he was referring to Raúl Mateu.

"I want to make it clear that I'm the client and I have a mind of my own," I said. "He can make his recommendations, but ultimately I call the shots."

I told him that I preferred to put a halt to the Selena mini-series until my contract was renewed. They filled the void by announcing another mini-series that was never produced.

At the end of the call, Ray promised that in two months he would sit with me to discuss the renewal of my contract and the purchase of the book's movie rights.

True to his word, Ray called me into his office exactly eight weeks later. He was with the company's head of business affairs, and in just a few minutes, they went through the general points of their proposed agreement.

It included a reasonable price for the book rights, a substantial salary boost, and an eye-popping six-figure signing bonus. Overall, the offer exceeded my expectations, and it made me feel validated, at last.

As Ray extended his arm to hand me the document, I reached out to grab it and told him how pleased I was.

"It all sounds good. There are only a couple of extra details that I would like to include, but Raúl can discuss that with both of you after he reviews it," I said.

Ray blew a fuse, which was out of character, because he is a true gentleman.

"Absolutely not," he said in a loud, agitated voice. "If he's part of the negotiation, there's no deal and there's no signing bonus!"

He took the document out of my hand and put it away.

I insisted. Raúl was my agent and I wanted him to review my contract. Ray reminded me that my contract with William Morris had lapsed. Therefore, I had no obligation to Raúl, legal or otherwise. He added that he didn't mind if I brought in a third party, as long as it wasn't Raúl. I replied that even though the contract had indeed expired, I had given Raúl my word, and my word was my contract. I would not stab him in the back, no matter how much money was at stake.

I can only speculate about why Ray had an issue with Raúl being part of the equation. Maybe he was still upset because Raúl had just negotiated a successful deal for another Univision personality. Maybe it was meant as a crippling blow so that Raúl wouldn't continue carving a niche in the Hispanic market, in which only a handful of TV stars used agents to negotiate their deals. Or maybe he truly felt that Raúl was giving me bad advice, and didn't want to lose me as a talent and friend.

Regardless of the reasons, the situation became tense and the head of business affairs intervened as the good cop. He suggested that I take twenty-four hours to reconsider.

Out of respect I told them I would, but the truth is that not even for a split second did I entertain the thought of accepting such terms.

As soon as I left the office, I wrote a note to Ray.

But I didn't send it until the next day.

It said simply, *I'm flattered by your generous offer, but you know me well enough to know I am not capable of such betrayal. If you understand my predicament, then you understand that I have no choice but to decline, until the time comes to negotiate my contract.*

That night I slept like a baby. I was at peace with myself. I had been both honest with Ray and loyal to Raúl. I never regretted giving up a signing-bonus check with so many zeros.

Six months later, when my contract was officially up for negotiation, the network executives did not try to negotiate with me. They knew it was not an option and called Raúl directly. Although they met several times, they couldn't reach an agreement. Univision was reluctant to grant me editorial say on my show, which to me was a key element, more so than the raise.

In March 2002, I drove off the Univision studios lot for the last time. Fifteen minutes later, as I stopped for gas, my cell phone rang. It was Ray.

"Mari, what are you doing? Come back now and let's settle this. What will it take? I have a blank check here with your name on it," he told me.

I really appreciated his call, but he was still missing the point, and I had too much respect for him to lead him on. My decision was final. It didn't matter if I was getting great ratings and was going to get a bigger check if, every day, I felt that my initiative was being squashed by the producers of my show.

When he realized my resolve, he got a bit mad. He must have assumed that I was going to the competition.

"Mari, you are a good seed, but a good seed needs sunlight to grow," he told me. "Univision is on the sunny side of the building and Telemundo is in the shade."

Gardening happens to be one of his hobbies, but I also know a little bit about plants.

"Thank you," I told him. "But you have to remember that there are some plants that blossom in the shade."

It was a leap of faith, but I knew it was the right thing. I signed with Telemundo, which was merging with media giant NBC, and launched my own show, *Al Rojo Vivo con María Celeste.* I was not only host but managing editor, a provision that Raúl had included in my contract. *Al Rojo Vivo* was competing head-to-head with my old show at Univision, forcing their producers to implement the changes I had suggested for so long. The *Los Angeles Times* called me "the most prominent player in a blossoming media experiment between two television networks in different languages."

Blossoming. How appropriate.

On the day of my five-year anniversary at Telemundo, the president of the network, Don Browne, threw a big party in my honor, which was attended by all the executives, the talent, and my staff. Raúl Mateu, my friend and agent, was there as well. And I wore a bright yellow dress, the color of the shining sun.

22

IF YOU WANT TO KEEP SOMETHING SECRET, DON'T EVEN TELL YOUR MOTHER.

My first crush was in first grade.

His name was Juan Carlos Romaguera, and I couldn't contain the overwhelming feelings I had for him.

He was a nice boy, but he certainly paid more attention to the girl sitting next to him than to me, although now I realize that it probably had more to do with logistics than love.

During a bathroom break, I stopped to have a drink of

water. A group of women was standing by the water fountain when I felt the need to reveal this all-consuming secret.

I don't know what possessed me to turn around and declare to the woman closest to me, "I'm in love with Juan Carlos Romaguera!" It felt good just to say it, to let one other person know the emotions that were swirling inside my young heart. But I soon regretted it.

"Oh my God, that's my son!" she responded.

I almost died. I certainly wanted to.

I might have died, actually, because I can't remember much else about the moment, except that the women all laughed and thought it was the cutest coincidence.

I didn't find it quite as amusing, especially after his mother spilled the beans to Juan Carlos and, out of shyness, he *really* started avoiding me.

That very day, that very moment, I learned that if you have something important and special, it's best to keep it to yourself. I can still recall the sick feeling in my stomach and my spinning head when my secret spilled. That single, pointed lesson from my childhood came in very handy more than three decades later. I had decided not to renew my contract with Univision, my employer of many years, and began negotiating with its rival, Telemundo.

For strategic reasons, nobody could know we were developing a new program that would compete directly with my former show and replace an existing Telemundo show in that same time slot. We didn't want to alert Univision, giving them time to react, and we also wanted to make sure that the in-house transition at Telemundo was as smooth as possible.

The top two Telemundo executives who masterminded the plan were very impressed that during the whole process I didn't share the news even with my mother, for fear that in her enthusiasm she might mention it to her friends, and eventually it would become public knowledge. Remembering Juan Carlos, I didn't tell a soul, even though I was bursting with excitement.

I had clandestine encounters with those two Telemundo executives in fancy hotel suites and even at my house. I wonder what people thought when they saw me acting so mysteriously with these two men, who made up a code name for me: "Diane." At the time, NBC was in the process of buying Telemundo, and in order to underscore the importance of bringing me in, the Telemundo execs explained to their future bosses, who didn't know me, that I was the Diane Sawyer of Hispanic television, and that hiring me would be a coup, comparable to NBC stealing Diane Sawyer from ABC.

Because of our discretion, no one ever found out until we decided it was time. On April 10, 2002, we made the official announcement in a luxurious Miami hotel, in a room full of journalists from all over the United States and Latin America. The event was broadcast live by Telemundo, and later I learned that everybody at Univision was glued to the television sets. They, too, were taken by surprise. Some executives were aghast and wondered if it was too late to regroup before the launching of my show two weeks later. But many of my former coworkers rejoiced at the news. They were happy for me, and also glad that this new challenge would force the producers of my former show to make changes that were long overdue. This also meant that there would be more competition, which was good for the industry.

Sometimes we succumb to the temptation to share with others those plans and feelings that are dear to our hearts. We have to learn that sometimes it may not be a good idea. Keeping your innermost dreams secret doesn't guarantee that they will come true. But it certainly gives them a fighting chance.

23

BE GRACIOUS WHEN OTHERS HAVE HARMED YOU.

It has taken me years to learn, but I think I now have the ability to move beyond hurtful memories.

I guess that is why I never dwelled on Octavio, the man who made my life hell during my first journalism job in the United States. Although I had been on the air as an anchor for just three months, Octavio came in with his own agenda and ideas about what was right for the station and eventually got rid of me without ever giving me a chance.

Those awful days, during which I was jobless and living alone in New York, seemed like a faded memory years later, especially on an amazing spring day in Miami when I was about to embark on a fantastic new venture.

I was hyperventilating backstage in a conference room at the Biltmore Hotel, listening to the presidents of NBC and Telemundo as they announced to the press the big news: I had been signed as the star and managing editor of a newsmagazine named after me, *Al Rojo Vivo con María Celeste,* which translates to "Red Hot Live with María Celeste." The expectations were enormous.

NBC's deal to buy Telemundo was just pending the government's approval and my show was going to be the first baby of this marriage. I was going to be working for both the Spanish- and English-speaking markets, on programs such as *Dateline* and the *Today* show.

Until very recently, I had been one of the main on-screen talents of Univision, Telemundo's rival, and after I left the network many were wondering what my next move would be. This was the answer they were waiting for.

I was taking deep breaths to calm my nerves when I heard the president of NBC explain over the microphone that this was a coup for Telemundo, equivalent to NBC landing the right to broadcast the Olympics. The pressure was on.

As I walked onstage, I was blinded by camera flashes and deafened by the thunderous applause. The event was being broadcast live and the room was packed with reporters. As I looked around, I saw many colleagues who had followed my career from day one. They were smiling and cheering, and that helped put me at ease.

I don't remember my speech, but I do recall being so excited that I grabbed the hands of both executives and lifted them up high, in a sign of victory. The crowd went crazy and so did the flashbulbs.

During the question-and-answer session, one journalist asked me point-blank: "You're considered the Katie Couric of Hispanic television. She makes about sixteen million dollars a year. Does your new salary reflect that?"

Being a veteran interviewer, I also know how to answer. "I will give you the parameters: I will be paying lots of taxes, but I'm making less than Katie Couric," I joked.

Another reporter asked what viewers could expect from my new show, and I responded with the catchy slogan that we had come up with to promote the launching: "Expect the unexpected."

After answering a few more questions, I posed for pictures and then bent down from the stage to shake hands with several journalists on the floor. That's when I saw him among the sea of reporters, the last person on the planet I expected to see: Octavio.

In an instant, I had a dozen flashbacks to the many times he blew me off and treated me condescendingly.

He stretched up his hand with a grin, and as I reached down to shake it, I could think only of the prophetic words that my ex-husband Guillermo said to me back in the Octavio days: *"He is on his way down, Mari. And you're on your way up."*

He was no longer the news director at the New York Univision affiliate. He had moved to Miami and was working as the editor of a minor magazine, a newspaper insert, which was a considerable step down.

Maybe he was there because he had to report on the event for his publication or wanted to be on good terms with Telemundo, supporting the network on such an important day. Maybe he was truly happy for me. There, in front of all our peers and the cameras, I could have given him the cold shoulder. This time around, I was in a more favorable situation. But the thought never crossed my mind. I had no desire to make him feel small, the way he once made me feel.

"Congratulations," he said, simply.

"Thanks for coming," I replied with a smile.

It felt good to have the opportunity to be the bigger person, to be gracious. I know that if I had wasted my time blaming Octavio and feeling sorry for myself, I wouldn't have been able to focus my energy on moving forward with my career to be on the stage that day.

I made a point of shaking Octavio's hand so he could see my sincerity: As far as I was concerned all may not have been forgotten, but all was forgiven.

Later that afternoon, it was announced that the merger between NBC and Telemundo had been approved, creating a new media giant in the Spanish-speaking world. It was all over the press the next morning, along with the news of my arrival at Telemundo. The headline in *The Washington Post* read: "NBC, Telemundo Snags Red Hot Arrarás from Univision." The story on the cover of *The Miami Herald* bore the headline "FCC Approves NBC's $2.7 Billion Purchase of

Telemundo—Telemundo Hires Talent from Rival." Under the headline was the picture of me with the presidents of Telemundo and NBC, our hands in the air in a sign of victory.

I imagined Octavio reading the article somewhere in the same city.

Life never ceases to amaze me. Talk about "Expect the unexpected."

24

PREJUDICE WILL BLIND YOU FROM SEEING THE WORLD AS IT REALLY IS.

There's nothing more liberating than allowing ourselves to see people as they really are, especially those we think of as different from us—someone of a different race or nationality, or of a different sexual orientation or religion, or someone with a different physical or mental ability.

Prejudice is a captor that blindfolds us and keeps us from seeing the world as it is. Sometimes it shouts at us with spite and vitriol. Other times, it whispers to us in hate-filled lullabies. But every time, these preconceived notions prevent us from opening our eyes and seeing reality. It is only after we lift the blindfold and filter out the noise that we are free to reach out to others, to discover the world and discover ourselves.

While working on a story, I had the chance to test how well I could overcome my prejudices.

I had read somewhere about the last leper colony in the continental United States, and I was intrigued. The sole mention of the word "leprosy" brought to mind images of what I had seen in the movies and read in the Bible. For centuries, lepers were considered "the untouchables," victims of an incurable disease that ate away at their flesh until their fingers and limbs fell off, turning them into disfigured monsters. It was a common belief that if you touched them, you would also be cursed for life.

I started to investigate and discovered that the facts were completely different. First of all, leprosy is one of the least contagious of all communicable diseases, and nowadays is treatable. It even has a different name: Hansen's disease, after the doctor who identified the bacteria that causes it. Thanks to a multidrug treatment that was developed from his findings, many people who are infected can now lead productive lives in society. Second, the disease is mostly transmitted by prolonged close contact with an infected person who is not under treatment.

Intent on doing a story, I traveled to the hospital and residential facility in Carville, Louisiana, that still housed a handful of patients. Some of them had been there for decades after being diagnosed and taken there forcibly, under court order. Others had been abandoned as children by their terrified families. Even though they were now free to leave, they had nowhere to go.

As I drove onto the former plantation, with its magnificent grounds lined with magnolia trees, I couldn't imagine how such a beautiful place could hide such a horrible past.

I was taken to the levee where the patients used to be brought in shackles on a barge, usually in the middle of the night. Some of the shackles were still there, serving as painful reminders of how the victims of this disease used to be condemned to a life of isolation.

I entered the mansion where most of the patients lived and was greeted by one of the residents, an elderly Hispanic man, who had been assigned as our guide. He extended his hand to greet me and for a second, I hesitated. Although rationally I knew that there was no risk of contagion, those old myths and unfounded fears came to mind. I shook his hand, which was missing the tips of some of the fingers.

As if reading my thoughts, he joked that I could squeeze his hand harder because it was not going to fall off. I liked him instantly.

He told me his story. He was brought to Carville when he was fourteen years old and he never left. Not once did his relatives come to visit. It was a traumatic experience that marked him more than the illness itself. “I grew up without a kiss or a hug. For years, no one touched me,” he confessed.

He took me on a tour of the cemetery on the property, where his “family”—the other patients he grew up with—were buried. There were only a few like him still living at the facility.

My cameraman and I had lunch with the rest of the residents, and their stories were very much the same. They were eager to tell the world how their lives had been stolen and how nobody cared. “Now, it is too late for me,” one old woman told me. “I am weak and penniless.” But what I gathered is that they were mostly afraid. Afraid of discovering that although time had passed, the world out there was still the same: afraid of them.

We spent the whole day together and when it was time

to part my heart ached. I knew that it would be a long time before they had another visitor. So this time I didn't wait for their cue. I kissed and hugged every single one of them good-bye.

As I walked over the threshold on my way out I felt a sense of accomplishment. Had I not challenged my own pre-conceptions I would have missed the opportunity to meet these wonderful people and learn about their unbelievable plight.

It's only when we're willing to set aside our narrow-mindedness that we can see people and the world as they really are.

The story I reported earned me an Emmy nomination, but the most important thing I won was freedom from the shackles of my own prejudice.

25

CHANGING THE WORLD FOR THE BETTER SHOULD BE ITS OWN REWARD.

I've always given little importance to awards.

In my career, I have been given more awards than I can think of, been invited to more banquets than I care to remember. And the funniest part is that, all too often, the awards themselves are so little about true achievement.

Yes, I have an Emmy, and that has a special place in my home. But there are two awards that have a special place in my heart, because they are about more than prestige and glamour; they are a reflection of standing up for what's right in our world.

I remember sitting on the couch one evening in 1994, flipping through the cable channels, when I came across an awards ceremony on the Discovery Channel. Engrossed, I watched as a group known as the Ark Trust Fund presented the Genesis Awards to members of the media for their roles in bringing animal rights issues to light. Prestigious news programs and well-known television personalities such as Hugh Downs received this honor for their work. They were added to a long list of past winners, including *Dateline NBC,* Peter Jennings, and *World News Tonight.* This was no dog-and-pony show (pardon the pun), not to me.

My husband, Manny, walked into the room as the credits were rolling, and I told him with conviction: "Next year, I'm going to be on that stage receiving one of those awards."

I was horrified by the abuses I had seen being denounced, but more than anything I was inspired to do the kind of work that would merit such an honor. And then, such a project literally landed in my lap. One of my television viewers wrote me a letter explaining that he had taken his family to a Mexican *charreada,* a traditional part rodeo, part fiesta, where he witnessed something horrible. In one of the performances, called a *coleada,* or "steer tailing," a man on horseback was supposed to grab the tail of a running steer, stop the animal in its tracks, and flip it on the ground. Instead, he ripped off the tail altogether, while the bloody animal writhed in pain. The viewer said his children were traumatized, and he asked me whether I could do something about it.

I started researching and discovered that this was not an isolated incident. Abuse was common both in Mexican and American rodeos. My staff and I debated doing a story on such a sensitive issue. Our audience is mostly Mexican and Mexican-American, and rodeos are part of their cultural tradition. But I pressed on, and insisted that if we did this sensitively, we could present this issue in a way that showed anyone who saw it the unmistakable abuses.

We spent weeks investigating and discovered that frequently horses were also tragically injured in the *charreadas.* In an event known as "horse tripping," participants demonstrate their mastery of the rope by lassoing the front legs of a running mare, which causes it to fall and, often, break both legs.

After weeks of investigation and having obtained graphic hidden camera videos to document the cruelty, both in the arena and behind closed doors, we aired a special series called

"In the Name of the Tradition." The response was amazing. Instead of a backlash against the show, thousands of viewers wrote and called in about how their eyes had been opened.

Shortly thereafter, I received a call from one of the directors of the Ark Trust Fund.

Weeks later, I was standing onstage receiving the Genesis Award for Outstanding Television News Feature. Manny was sitting in the audience and we exchanged a knowing glance: It was exactly a year after I had first learned about the awards.

The inscription on the plaque read: "To María Celeste Arrarás, whose groundbreaking, courageous and uncompromising account challenging horse abuse in the guise of 'sport' has increased public understanding of animal issues."

That recognition only served to deepen my awareness and made me realize how many people shared my passion. One of those people sat across from me in the newsroom. Irma Negroni, the head writer of my show and a trusted friend, brought to my attention something she had just read in a newspaper about Puerto Rico. Islanders were outraged by the treatment of seven polar bears at the hands of a traveling circus that kept the Arctic animals in cages at the side of the road under the scorching tropical sun. Some of the bears were struggling to breathe and could barely hold their heads up.

The heat had made them lose a third of their body fat and shed big patches of fur.

We came up with a plan. We did a story on the plight of the polar bears in Puerto Rico. After the story was broadcast on my show throughout the United States and Latin America, media outlets from all over the world picked up on it, and it became a huge controversy—just as we knew it would.

Several journalists from the island called to interview me, eager to know my opinion. I spoke both as a journalist and as a fellow Puerto Rican. I denounced the situation and called for action against the circus. Public condemnation became stronger as the bears grew weaker. Federal authorities intervened and, after completing their investigation, seized the bears. Unfortunately, it was too late for one of the animals, which died en route to her new home in a U.S. sanctuary.

That whole episode made it evident that to prevent this from happening again, stronger laws were needed. I decided to take advantage of my notoriety on the island and called for a regulation that would deny entry to circuses featuring animals. I personally called the speaker of Puerto Rico's House of Representatives, who agreed to draft a proposal to be submitted to Congress. Then I contacted the president of the Senate and every single congressperson on their cell phones, seeking their support for the bill. When the public hearings were held, I traveled to San Juan to testify. There was a media frenzy, and when I presented my case, which was supported by hidden-camera videos of the abuse inflicted upon circus animals, some of the legislators were brought to tears.

Unfortunately, the proposal never made it to the floor for voting—thanks to a last-minute intervention by powerful lobbyists for the circus industry.

But the People for the Ethical Treatment of Animals recognized my effort and honored me with their Humanitarian award that year. I invited Irma, who had been my right hand in this initiative, to join me at the Waldorf-Astoria in New York, where the awards banquet was held. It was exciting; we met Paul McCartney, Pamela Anderson, Charlize Theron, and the lead singer of The Pretenders, Chrissie Hynde.

Minutes before my acceptance speech, I was flipping through a pamphlet about all the causes PETA was fighting against. In those pages, I saw the name of a company I had just signed a contract to endorse. I had no clue that that company was engaging in cruel practices. And as they called my name to come up on stage, all I could think was "How am I going to get out of this contract?"

Then I read the inscription on the black lacquer plaque

with a perfect white dove: "For your heartfelt dedication to educating the public about animal abuse."

That night, I phoned my agent and called off the deal.

There are things in this world that are more meaningful than money. One of them is speaking out on behalf of the weak and the voiceless. You should do it selflessly and at every opportunity. Who knows—in the end, you may be rewarded with more than just a good feeling.

26

RESENTMENT IS A HEAVY ANCHOR THAT CAN WEIGH YOU DOWN AND DROWN YOU.

When somebody stops loving you, the hardest thing to do is to accept it and move on. It's one of those things in life that you will want to change and won't be able to. But you can change the way you feel about it, and that is just as good.

It took my mother more than a decade to make peace with the other woman. The woman she blamed for the end of her marriage, and who my father took as his bride three months after their divorce. We found out about the wedding from the newspaper. As we were having breakfast, there it was, on top of the table on the front page: the new Mrs. Arrarás, dressed in white. My father was running for mayor of San Juan, so his wedding was big news.

I don't recall how my mother reacted, but I do remember how I felt—like my world had come to an end. Every child dreams of seeing their parents together and I knew, there and then, that reconciliation was no longer possible. I was eleven years old.

The worst part was that I couldn't even vent to my dad. For months, I refused to talk to him, upset at his decision to leave and date another woman before I was able to deal with the shock of the separation. I wanted him to feel my pain.

Even though I was closer to him than to my mother, I took her side. How could I not? I was hurting so badly, and I dealt with it by punishing my father and making my new stepmother's life miserable. It became my mission. At first, I wouldn't even look at Luissette, much less call her by name. For almost two years, when I addressed her I would just say "Hey, you!" When I visited them, I would challenge her every step of the way. If she said yes, I said no. My mother couldn't have been more proud of me.

Then things took a turn. My mom remarried, and when her husband accepted a job in New Jersey, they moved. My sister and I were in the middle of the school year and it was decided that we would stay in Puerto Rico with my father. I found, despite myself, that there were things to like about "Hey, you." She was kind and patient with me in spite of my insolence. I began to realize that she put up with me because she truly loved my father. She didn't try to replace my mother. And that won me over.

My mother became insanely jealous. Not only had she lost my father, but now she felt that Luissette was also stealing me. So when she would call from New Jersey and I would make a nice comment about my stepmother or my new siblings, she would get mad at me. Her fear of being replaced continued for years.

Even though my mom traveled to the island often to see us, she avoided Luissette like the plague. I would be racked with anxiety just thinking about their next encounter. My mother went as far as refusing to attend important events, even my wedding, just because Luissette was going to be there. She failed to see that her attitude was alienating her from me and pushing me closer to my stepmother. My mother became her own worst enemy. She knew this, but she was trapped by her inability to forgive.

And Luissette did try. After the first rocky years, she reached out to my mom. "Astrid, don't fight with her, I know Mari loves you very much. Make good use of the time you have together," she would tell my mother.

It must have been difficult for my mother at the beginning to hear advice from Luissette, and to accept that I came to love her like a second mother. It took many years—too many—but in time she did, and my stepmother and mother actually became friends.

I thought about those days a lot after my second husband, Manny, left me.

I found out that he had been having an affair thanks to my dear friend and coanchor at *Primer Impacto,* Myrka Dellanos. She took me to our office and said that she had something very painful to tell me. By her expression, I thought the worst: Had something happened to my kids?

"No," she replied.

The night before, she began, she had been having a drink with her husband at a club when a young woman who recognized her from television approached her. The stranger introduced herself and said she was a fan of our show, and that she liked me very much. Then she dropped the bomb.

"I feel very sorry for María Celeste, because I work with her husband's girlfriend and he comes to visit her all the time," she told Myrka. "He even took her to Chicago not long ago."

That's when Myrka knew that this wasn't just malicious gossip.

Weeks before, I had confided in her about how upset I was that Manny had gone on a business trip to Chicago, even though Miami was under a hurricane alert and I was worried about staying home alone with our three small children, two of whom were still in diapers. All the pieces of the puzzle fell into place. I understood why he had been coming home late at night, why he often turned off his cell phone, why he seemed so distant.

I felt a rush of anxiety and my mind started racing. I couldn't even stay long enough to express my gratitude to Myrka for telling me the truth. I told the producer in charge that I had a personal emergency and took off. The "informant" had given Myrka her phone number and I dialed it from the road. She told me everything she knew and it was more than I cared to find out. But I thanked her.

I arrived at my husband's office and called him from the car to let him know I was downstairs. It was five minutes before the start of my show, so he figured that something was very wrong.

"Mari, is there a problem?" he asked.

"Yes, and it has a name: Selene."

There was a long silence.

"I'll be right down," he said.

We drove a few blocks and parked in an empty lot, where he admitted to the affair. He said that he had met her at the gym and had been seeing her for the last five months. He said he was relieved that I had found out because he was tired of living a double life and that, for a while, he had wanted to end it but didn't know how. I asked him if he loved her and he said that he loved me.

I believed him and forgave him, because I loved him, too.

But we never stood a chance, because he had not been completely honest with me. In reality, the affair had started shortly after I had become pregnant with our daughter, Lara, more than a year and half before. So Selene was not willing to give him up that easily. After he broke the relationship off, she insisted, and he was weak.

When I began to suspect that Selene was still in the picture I did what many women do: I fought with Manny. All it did was push him further into her arms, and it became a battle of me against them, and, in the process, they fell in love.

After trying for a year to save our marriage, he left me two days after Christmas in December 2002. I felt directionless and devastated for a few months. Then I became angry and resentful during our bitter divorce. At first, I acted the same way I did when I was a child and didn't want to lose my dad to Luissette: I resisted. But I learned from my parents' divorce that I had no choice but to accept the inevitable and live with it. Nothing I could do was going to change the final outcome.

On the day Manny was to remarry, I invited a girlfriend over for dinner. We talked about what my life would be from now on, what it had been like when I was a young girl. I thought of my mother, and how our relationship had faltered when she maintained her resentment. Would I, too, be part of a war in which I was the only soldier?

I thought about my children, who would wonder how they should treat my ex-husband's new bride, and I realized that they would look to me for their cues, as I had looked to my mother. I took my phone from my purse and sent my ex-husband a simple text message.

"Congratulations on your wedding," I typed. "I hope it works out for you. I'm sure if you're making this decision, it's the right one."

A few minutes later, my phone beeped.

"Thank you, Mari," Manny responded. "I know you mean it."

A month after Manny and Selene were married, my ex-husband's family, who had been my family for more than ten years and, in many ways, still was, hosted Christmas Eve dinner, and we were all invited. We all played dominoes together, talked, joked, ate at the same table. The next month was our daughter's birthday, and I invited them to my house to celebrate. His wife took pictures of me posing with my children, and they were all smiling.

I knew that that was how I wanted my kids to feel about the people who loved them. Whatever had happened between their father and me was not greater than the love we had for them. I know that if I had continued this war, my kids would have suffered. And the one who would have suffered the most would have been me. Manny and Selene would have gone on to live a happy life and I would have stayed behind, imprisoned in a life of bitterness. I wanted to give myself a chance to live. And I wanted my children to see me do that.

Selene and I later spoke about the tumultuous journey each of us had lived through. We came to understand each other better and it helped us get along well.

I wondered what my mother would think—she who had devoted so much energy to resisting the curves life had thrown her. Once, over coffee, she told me.

"I'm so proud of you, Mari," she said. "I wish I could have gotten over it sooner, like you did, rather than later."

It was only after I began charting a new course that I was able to accept the turbulent seas I fought so strongly against. And in the end, I made peace with the storm. Resentment is an anchor that keeps you from moving forward and sinks everyone who reaches out to help you. Let go of the weight and set yourself free.

27

NOTHING IS HARDER THAN THE SOFTNESS OF INDIFFERENCE.

There's no doubt that when we truly want something, we can be relentless. Yet sometimes, when we try too hard, it can have the opposite effect: The more we pursue, the more elusive our goal becomes.

When we let go, it often find its way to us.

I began to understand that concept during my teenage years, around the time when I was dreading to be a debutante.

The idea of celebrating my "Quinces"—my fifteenth

birthday, similar to a Sweet 16 for an American girl—had very little appeal for me. I thought it was a passé tradition, corny and tacky. Plus, there was the issue of finding a date. I was attending an all-girls school in my native Puerto Rico, so there was no chance of casually running into a boy and asking him to be my companion. It would take an actual phone call.

After my stepmother, Luissette, lobbied me for months, I decided to go along with the torture, and I agreed to participate in the Quinceañero that the Caparra Country Club was celebrating for the girls that year. But soon after I agreed, I discovered that the torture came in a double dosage. In addition to having the actual party, there was to be a Baile de Confirmación, where they announce that year's debutantes—a sort of dance before the dance. Now I needed *two* dates! That meant *two* excruciating phone calls, leaving myself open to two possible rejections, if not more.

While my stepmother spent her days figuring out what I was going to wear for both occasions, I spent endless nights trying to figure out whom to invite as my partner to the Baile de Confirmación. When I decided on one particular boy, I still didn't have the courage to call him myself. So I asked one of my girlfriends to impersonate me. I've always had a very distinct, deep voice, so it was foolish to think that anyone would believe she was me, but I didn't care. Anything was better than having to confront my own teenage insecurity and fear of rejection. I was glad I didn't make the phone call myself because, as it turned out, the boy in question already had a date.

So I went solo to my Baile de Confirmación. I wore my first designer dress ever, a gray chiffon strapless with a beautiful peach satin bow at the waist. At the party I hung out with my friend Celestino Arias. He had recently broken up with his girlfriend and also was there alone. We joked about being namesakes, Celestino and Celeste, and danced the night away. That night there was chemistry between us, and, to my surprise, *he* asked *me* that night if he could be my date for the Quinceañero.

What a relief, I thought. *I finally have someone with whom to dance the waltz.*

For the first time, I actually felt enthusiastic about the Quinceañero. For the next few days I was very gung-ho. I even went to my dress fittings without complaining. Celestino and I worked out all the details, down to the color corsage I was going to wear.

Then he dropped the bomb.

Two days before the party, he called to say he had gotten back with his girlfriend and had to cancel.

I was dumbfounded and went into a panic.

I had forty-eight hours to find a date. Feeling sorry for me, my close friends mobilized their network and found me a blind date—the blind date from hell!

We met the night of the party and from the first moment there was not a spark of fireworks on either side. I handed him the tickets, which cost about $150 each, and the second we went in, we went our separate ways. I never spoke to him or saw him again for the rest of the night. To this day, I don't remember his name. All I remember is seeing Celestino and his girlfriend on the dance floor, cheek to cheek. She gave me one of those "I've got him and you don't" looks, and I left soon after.

I learned later that when his girlfriend found out that Celestino and I had been together at the Baile de Confirmación, she felt a renewed interest in him. She spent the next two weeks playing coy with him, ignoring him when they bumped into each other. And it worked like a charm.

The following year Celestino reappeared in my life. It was two months before his high school graduation and he was no longer with his girlfriend. He asked me to be his date for a dance in honor of the graduates receiving their class rings. Since I had no romantic feelings for him and we had been good friends before that Quinceañero fiasco, I accepted.

A couple of weeks went by and I had just gotten home late one Friday night from hanging out with my friends when my phone rang. It was Celestino and he was frantic.

Turns out the class ring dance was that Friday. I had completely forgotten. He had been by my house twice earlier that night to pick me up.

"I've been looking all over for you! What do you mean standing me up like that?" he said.

I paused for a moment.

"I call it an eye for an eye," I said.

He was silent for a second, and then he responded like a good sport:

"Touché."

We both broke out laughing, and I quickly told him the real reason why I missed our date. Revenge was the farthest thing from my mind. I simply forgot to write it in my calendar.

Maybe because I was so sincere, but more likely because I was indifferent to his invitation, he took an interest in me and asked me out a couple of times after that. But by then I saw him only as a friend and we remained as such.

The whole episode taught me a big lesson about how human beings love the thrill of the chase. The unfortunate truth is that most of us tend to value that which escapes us, and in the process we may lose someone truly valuable.

Years later, when I had a love-struck child of my own, I thought about Celestino. My son Adrian, eight at the time, had a crush on a classmate who was ignoring him, and he was dejected. He asked me for some advice and I simply told him, "Ignore her back."

For two weeks he followed my instructions like a soldier until he came back, smiling, to report, "Bianca kind of likes me now."

I remembered something my paternal grandmother used to tell me: "Nothing is harder than the softness of indifference."

It always works like a charm.

28

NEVER LET A BAD EXPERIENCE ROB YOU OF YOUR FAITH IN HUMANITY.

Throughout your life, you will be confronted over and over with a sad truth: Some of the people you love and trust will disappoint you. There is nothing you can do about it and you can't build immunity to it. It will hurt every time. Yet you can never let these unfortunate betrayals steal your capacity to open up and believe in others.

One of the most unexpected disappointments of my life came at the hands of a woman I will call Nadia Gómez. I'd rather not use her real name for the sake of her son, who is still a young boy. Despite everything she did to me, I don't wish to cause her any more harm than the harm she has caused herself.

We met one afternoon in October 1997 when I was six months pregnant with my son Julian. She was also expecting and waiting in line behind me to pay for some items at a Babies R Us store in Miami. She introduced herself and said she recognized me from my show *Primer Impacto,* where I was the coanchor. She came across as very nice and extroverted, so I took an immediate liking to her. We talked briefly about our pregnancies and what she did for a living.

She said she was working as an assistant to one of the best-known pitchers in baseball and a star in Miami, Alex Fernandez, who had helped the Florida Marlins win their first World Series title. According to her, she was his liaison to the media and trusted assistant in charge of coordinating his busy calendar and even paying his personal bills. Nadia sounded very efficient, and it made me wish that I had someone like her to help me on a daily basis.

I said good-bye expecting never to see her again.

Then, four years later, I got a phone call. I didn't recognize her voice or her name, but when she reminded me of our brief encounter at the baby store years ago, I immediately remembered Nadia Gómez. She had read in *The Miami Herald* that I was in the middle of negotiating my contract with Univision and wanted to wish me luck. "If by any chance you get to hire an assistant as part of your new deal, please consider me," she said. "I would be very interested in the position." As a matter of fact, one of the items on my wish list for the new contract was a stipulation that allowed me to have an assistant.

What an incredible coincidence! I thought.

Four months later, after I decided to leave Univision and join Telemundo, I formally interviewed her. We had chemistry, and I hired her on the spot.

Nadia was by my side during the creation of my new show *Al Rojo Vivo with María Celeste* from day one. She was unconditionally supportive, loyal, there whenever I needed her. She would act as my eyes and ears, telling me who was a team player and who wasn't. And I relied on her input.

I was consumed with work, and when she proved that she could get things done, I started giving her more responsibilities. It seemed that she could almost foresee what I was going to need, and before I verbalized it, it was done. She was in charge of my agenda and coordinated everything I had to do so that I could concentrate on the show. Because it was a new project, I was working fourteen hours a day, so I was grateful that, thanks to her, my personal things were in order. She made me feel as if there was nothing in the world I had to worry about.

When my second husband, Manny, left the house in December 2002, I was devastated, but somehow I managed to go to work every day. It took every ounce of discipline I had to get up from bed and not stay at home, depressed. At Telemundo I would lock myself in my office to work on the computer so that no one would see my face twisted in grief. Nadia was the only one who could come in and out without an invitation. I was grateful that she acted as a buffer between me and the outside world, which seemed too painful to join.

When the divorce proceedings began, there was a lot of animosity between Manny and me. Nadia knew that I dreaded having to go to his office, where my bills and personal mail were still being delivered. So I was touched when she offered to pick up my mail at his office every week.

Nadia made me feel that I could count on her during that emotionally overwhelming period when I didn't have the peace of mind to deal with the mundane. She began managing the payment of my bills so that I wouldn't stress over paperwork and numbers. It was a huge relief and I welcomed her initiative. The last thing I wanted to worry about was telephone and utility bills. It seemed that she was ready to take care of all the issues I wanted to run away from as I attempted to balance work and my children in the face of the divorce.

She did little things that made a big difference. When I lost my cell phone the morning I was to leave on a trip, she got me a replacement in record time and had it delivered to me just in time for my flight. I was already on the plane when it rang and I saw the caller ID: "Nadia Gómez." She had even programmed it with her contact information. When I thanked her, she replied, "Mine is the only number you need to know. I'll take care of everything for you."

And she did. If I needed to buy clothes for the show, she would go online and print out some suggestions for me. I would tease her that she was a professional Internet shopper.

When there was a problem she would always solve it. My salon stopped taking credit cards, she said, so she wrote out checks for me before my appointments, including the tip and taxes, calculated down to the last cent. That way I wouldn't waste my precious time at the cashier. She was one of a kind.

Nadia became my confidante, especially during that vulnerable time. I would share with her every excruciating detail of the divorce and ask her for advice. But mostly I just needed someone to talk to. And Nadia filled that role. We became such close friends that the first Christmas after my separation, Nadia and her husband invited me to go with them to New York for a weekend. I wasn't able to make it but I was moved by the invitation. They would send me flowers for my birthday and bought all kinds of gifts for my kids on a visit to Disney World. They sort of became my extended family.

That's why I was so happy for them when her husband opened a pet shop and, it seemed, they started doing really well right from the start. They were able to upgrade their cars, and Nadia started to buy nice clothes and jewelry. She was brand savvy, unlike me. I remember receiving a gold heart pendant one year as a Valentine's Day gift, and she immediately informed me that it was Chopard. Very expensive, she said.

I was glad to see Nadia revamping herself. When she got hair extensions like mine, cut her hair just like mine, and colored it the same shade of red, one of my friends commented that she was turning into my clone. I saw no harm in that; I thought Nadia wanted to imitate me because she looked up to me. I was flattered by it.

With the divorce nearly complete, in the winter of 2004, I was ready to reemerge and take charge of my finances, which

I had neglected. I asked Nadia to set up appointments with my accountant and financial adviser, and to call the credit card companies to make sure they started mailing the monthly statements to my home address. When Nadia couldn't get something accomplished immediately, she felt bad. "Can you believe it takes three months for the credit cards to actually make a change of address?" she would say. She would also take it personally when people would cancel an appointment at the last minute, and both my financial adviser and my accountant were doing that frequently. If it wasn't one it was the other. Thank God Nadia was on top of it.

As part of her reinvention, she underwent plastic surgery in February 2005 and took two weeks off. Her time off was good for me, too. It allowed me to take control of my bills. For more than a year and a half, I had stopped opening the bills and bank statements and just handed all my correspondence to Nadia. I found a stack on top of her desk, *poor thing,* and started going through them.

The first envelope I opened was my bank statement. At first, I was glad to see a transaction for $19,000, the approximate amount I was due back from my credit card company for a trip to the Orient I had canceled, having planned to take it with my ex-husband. But as I looked more closely, I noticed it wasn't a refund. It was a withdrawal. It was used to pay my credit card company.

I called the credit card company and they said the online transfer was used to pay my many charges. "What were they?" I asked. The customer service agent read the first one. It was for a purchase from an Internet store, Amazon.com. It struck me as an error, since I never purchased things online. When I said I wanted to dispute that store's charge, the receptionist asked, "Which one? There are more than twenty."

There is a moment—you know the one. The moment in so many Hollywood mystery thrillers when the police detective learns that the killer he is chasing has been right under his nose all along. I felt that moment, felt the camera zoom in on my face as reality began washing over me. The credit card receptionist began reading off dozens and dozens of Internet purchases, hundreds if she went back months. Tens of thousands of dollars were racked up every month, paid in full by wire transfers from my bank account. And my mind went to the person who had been standing beside me in my worst of times: Nadia.

I spent the next few hours canceling all my credit cards, alerting my bank to the fraud. Then I called the authorities. They advised me not to let her know that I knew. She might try to hide evidence or even try to leave the country. So I had to place a call to Nadia Gómez worthy of an Oscar. She answered the phone from her bed, where she was still convalescing from the cosmetic surgery. I very sweetly asked how she was feeling and told her in passing that someone had run off with my wallet while I was at dinner. When I volunteered that thank God all I had was a few dollars and my credit cards, there was silence.

After a couple of seconds Nadia offered to contact the credit card companies to cancel the stolen cards and issue new ones.

"No, no, no, you're recovering," I said. "Besides, I've already canceled all the cards."

This time there was a long silence that told me all I needed to know.

Nadia was arrested the next morning. When questioned by the detectives, she alleged that every single item she charged to my credit cards had been ordered by me. Luckily, I was a size four and she was a size eight. All the designer clothes that she had ordered online from stores like Neiman Marcus and Saks Fifth Avenue were a size eight. So it became obvious that she was lying.

When the authorities executed a search warrant at her

house, they discovered boxes and boxes of unopened merchandise. Everything had been charged to my credit cards.

In her wallet they found a Capitol One credit card with her name on it. She had opened the account by forging my signature and had added herself and her husband as authorized users. She used that particular credit card to pay for the remodeling of her kitchen.

The agents from the white-collar crime unit also found several batches of receipts totaling tens of thousands of dollars charged to my American Express card by the Pet Shop company owned by Nadia's husband. They confiscated the Point of Sale Terminal unit that was used to make the unauthorized charges.

According to one of the detectives, they also found firearms and a Santeria altar that supposedly had my picture on it.

It took me months to unravel the complex financial web designed by Nadia to rob me of approximately $300,000 in a year and a half. I was determined to build a strong case against her and discover the extent of the fraud. I spent about six hours a day on the phone with the credit card companies, the investigators, and the merchants, poring over bills and documents. In the process I found out that Nadia let some of my insurance policies lapse so that she could get her hands on the money.

You may ask yourself how I could be so naïve and not realize that my bank account was being drained. She had a clever system set up. Every month she would ask me to write a check for my credit cards for the total amount of my bona fide expenses. The amount always agreed with what I estimated I had spent, so it never raised suspicions. Little did I know that the moment I turned around, she would tear up the check and go on to pay both my legitimate charges and hers via wire transfer from my bank account. Unbeknownst to me, she had set up online access to my credit card accounts and would monitor them religiously. Just before she reached the credit limit, she would pay them.

My accountant and my financial adviser were shocked, too. As it turns out, it was Nadia who had been calling to cancel the meetings with them. She wanted me isolated and under her control so she could continue the financial rape.

I realized that she had tried to match my hairstyle because she began to believe that she was me. And what about those checks for the hair salon, calculated to the last cent? Those were also part of her scheme. She had to make sure I never used my credit card because she went to the same salon and was charging her own expenses to my credit card. She never presented the actual card but provided them with the number that she had copied on a Post-it note, saying that the card belonged to her husband and she was authorized to use it. Because she was my trusted assistant, and I have been going to the same place for years, no one questioned her.

I was appalled to discover that I had paid for the flower arrangements she had sent me for my birthday. I had also paid for all her recent family vacations and her weekend escapade with her husband to New York—the one they had invited me to, to cheer me up in the midst of my divorce.

The one that took the cake was her alleged weekend trip to Disney World that never happened. The week before, she called in sick but assured me that I could reach her at any time on her cell. I did call her a few times to see how she was feeling and was happy to hear that she felt good enough to go to Orlando with her family. In reality, she had gone to the Bahamas for a week at my expense, having all her calls, including those well-wishes from me, forwarded to a satellite phone she also rented with my credit card. She had lied about her health to justify her absence from the office. Nadia had been planning this for a long time, going to the extreme of ordering presents for my children on Disney.com a month before, all charged to one of my credit cards. The gifts gave credence to her charade.

The theft included things great and small. I ended up paying for her son's birthday party at a Miami bowling alley, and even for his four-dollar lunch at Burger King.

It took me a while to figure out how she had managed to siphon thousands of dollars in cash advances from a Visa card I carried with me all the time, until I looked deeper. Turns out that all the cash had been withdrawn from the same ATM machine, located at Telemundo, between five and six in the afternoon when I was live on the air. That meant that Nadia would go into my wallet, take the card, make her withdrawal, and return it before the show was over.

She had been making credit card purchases until the last possible second, even charging from her recovery bed after plastic surgery. After she was arrested, her husband used the cell phone I had been unknowingly paying for to call a bail bondsman for her.

Eventually, Nadia came to an agreement with the Florida State Attorney's office. To avoid jail time, she pleaded guilty to the charges of grand theft and identity theft. She also agreed to repay most of the money she had taken from me. I saw her for the last time on the day that she was sentenced to five years' probation. She didn't seem remorseful or embarrassed. And not once did she look at me.

When I left the courthouse, check in hand, I felt neither happy nor victorious. To me, it was just a cold business transaction. I never shed a single tear over Nadia's betrayal because I realized that the Nadia I trusted and cared for never existed.

Needless to say, the event was educational, a lesson that ignorance is not bliss but rather a brutal teacher. I overcame my discomfort with the Internet and learned to oversee all of my finances. I had let my life spiral out of control, choosing to close my eyes rather than face all my challenges. Any time you do that, I learned, you will eventually pay the price.

But I didn't let the experience sour me on people. What Nadia had stolen from me, money could replace. However, I would not let her steal my faith in humanity—for that is priceless.

29

EVEN IF YOU WANT TO SELL MAGAZINES, DON'T SELL YOUR SOUL.

Many people dream of one day being on the cover of a magazine. And there was a time when I shared that dream. I never would have guessed that, over time, I would end up on not just one, but more than a hundred different covers. Nor that I would actually turn down an opportunity to do the cover of *People en Español.* I did it because I firmly believe that it is our duty to take strong stands for what we believe in, even if it means passing up a great opportunity.

It was January 2006 when I received a phone call from the editor of *People en Español,* with whom I had developed a close friendship after having been featured on the publication's cover more than a dozen times. He wanted me for the cover of an upcoming issue that was going to be called "The Five TV Divas," featuring the most popular female personalities in Hispanic television.

I was apprehensive about the title because the word "diva" has a negative connotation. People associate the term with stars who are difficult, demanding, and have a chip on their shoulder. Still, in a very undivalike decision, I accepted the offer without even asking who else was going to be on the cover.

For me, the most important consideration was to show *People en Español* that I appreciated their support throughout the years. So even when I found out that some of the other celebrities who would appear on the cover were far less established than I was, I still kept my commitment. I didn't mind sharing the limelight.

At the request of some of the divas, the photo shoot had to be rescheduled a couple of times. And every time I went along with it. But one conversation changed the picture.

A week before the shoot, I received a call from the folks at *People* to finalize the details. I would be on the cover of the edition sent to subscribers and on the edition for sale on the stands. They also said they would be filming behind-the-scenes footage of the photo session and that they would provide my show with a promotional video clip and a "Telemundo-friendly cover."

I knew what that meant.

Even though I work at Telemundo, having worked for Univision I know for a fact that the company has a policy of not giving any airtime to magazine covers that feature talent from other networks. So all Hispanic magazines, *People* included, had a tough choice to make: edit their covers or not get airtime on the number one Spanish-language network. In this case, *People* chose to do mock covers for promotional purposes only: one featuring only the Univision divas and another one with the Telemundo divas.

"We don't need a Telemundo-friendly cover," I responded. "We don't believe in manipulating reality."

One of the reasons I had decided to join Telemundo was precisely because they were fair and didn't practice censorship. If I went along with the project I would be condoning

Univision's unfair practice. And so I told *People* that I could no longer be part of the divas issue.

I worried that this could jeopardize my relationship with the magazine, but something larger was at stake. I believe that if you're an industry giant, like Univision, you have to be a gentle giant. Putting magazines under that kind of pressure not only hinders fair competition among the networks, but also curtails the possibility of young talent on rival networks getting much-needed exposure. It's unethical.

To my surprise the decision I made stole the headline. The cover read, "The Divas of Television: Five together, and one absent." In a sidebar titled "Where is María Celeste?" the magazine graciously allowed me to explain my reason for not attending. "I feel that someone should be chosen to be on the cover based on their merit and accomplishments, not what network they are affiliated with," they quoted me as saying.

I was even more surprised when, for the following issue, *People en Español* asked me to be on the cover—alone.

That incident only served to reinforce my belief that when you act according to principles and are honest about your motives, people respect you. Regardless of the final outcome, you have to speak out and stay true to your convictions.

We can never know how these things will turn out, and you should never do something expecting vindication. But the universe does have a way of conspiring to reward you for doing the right thing.

30

YOU'LL KNOW IT'S REAL LOVE WHEN YOU'RE WILLING TO SACRIFICE LOBSTER FOR TUNA FISH.

Few things in this world can provoke more anxiety than knowing that the person you love is dating someone else.

Yet more likely than not, we all have to live through that horrible experience at least once in our lives.

I lost count of how many times I've lived through it, starting with my first puppy love in first grade. But I do remember when I learned how to cope with it. It was in the early 1980s, when I was a sophomore in college.

I had been dating my first boyfriend, Vince, for about two years, when on Valentine's Day (of all days!) he decided to break up with me. He wanted the chance to meet "other people." Typical.

I took it as a personal rejection and vowed to hate Valentine's Day from that day forward.

I felt even more hurt after I learned that Vince was going to be the guest of honor at a swanky lobster bash hosted by the rich New Orleans family of a girl named Liz, who had always had a thing for him.

The night of the feast I was restless, anxious, and not very hungry. Yet I opened a can of tuna fish and made a salad to nibble on, mostly to kill time.

I couldn't stop asking myself what was wrong with me. *What did she have that I didn't?* I wished that my family lived in New Orleans so that I could have extended a similar invitation to Vince. More than anything, I wished I hadn't lost him to someone else.

I was imagining all kinds of love scenarios and romantic conversations between Vince and Liz when my apartment doorbell rang.

It was him.

He grabbed me and gave me a bear hug and a big kiss. I was confused and speechless but he saw the question in my eyes: Wasn't he supposed to be somewhere else?

"I'd rather eat tuna with you than lobster with Liz," he said with a mischievous smile.

I knew it was a line. Maybe he did, too. But I've never had a better time during an uneventful weekend than I did sharing tuna salad with him as we watched TV. Since then, I have come to believe there is great merit in the "lobster or tuna" test: Would I rather go have a fancy meal with someone else, or stay home on a lazy Saturday night with this person? If you ever doubt whether you want to be with someone, put him or her to that litmus test.

You'll know right away.

I remembered that incident many years later, after my second divorce. I had fallen madly in love with someone who had also recently divorced. We were having a heart-to-heart talk over pizza and a bottle of wine when he told me how happy he felt in spite of the simplicity of the night. In the last stages of his failed marriage, he told me, he had gone to Paris with his wife in an attempt to salvage their ailing relationship. He realized it was all over when he found himself staring at the walls of his luxurious five-star hotel room, in one of the most romantic cities in the world, while she read a book.

I realized that in spite of his immaturity and the heartbreak he caused me, Vince taught me a very important lesson that night so many years ago:

You don't need any trimmings when love is the main course.

31

IT'S THE LITTLE PEOPLE WHO CAN MAKE THE BIGGEST DIFFERENCE.

Almost every time I'm interviewed, I get asked the same question: "Who is the most interesting person you have ever interviewed?"

Time and time again, I give the same response: "There is not one single person, there are many. And none of them are famous."

Regular people are usually much more interesting. They are not guarded like manufactured celebrities. They speak openly without having to first consult their public relations team, and they usually have better stories to tell.

I call them the anonymous heroes. And one of my favorites is Don Pachico Mayoral. While I was working my first assignment for NBC's *Nightly News* in March 2008, he taught me—and the world, for that matter—that a single person can make a difference.

It was more than forty years ago that Don Pachico was fishing in the waters of San Ignacio Lagoon, in Baja California, Mexico, when a great dark figure broke the plane of the deep blue ocean. A massive gray whale took him by surprise. It appeared first on one side of his small boat, then on the other. He trembled as the great animal appeared and disappeared below the surface of the water.

For some reason, the whale was very insistent, as if it wanted to get Don Pachico's attention. They made eye contact, and the next time it got close to the side of his boat, he ventured to touch it. To his amazement, the whale did not flinch. In fact, it seemed to enjoy it. He stayed there for more than forty minutes, caressing the gentle giant until it finally swam off.

This contact between man and sea creature was no small act. As far as anyone knew, Don Pachico was the first person ever to touch a gray whale in the wild and live to tell about it.

For decades, gray whales were known as Devil Fish. They had been known to violently attack, capsize, and destroy any boat in sight. And with good reason: The gray whale was hunted to the brink of extinction at the turn of the century.

After his close encounter, Don Pachico was convinced not only that this was a noble animal, but that it was capable of forgiving man for having hunted it so intently for generations.

While I was working on Don Pachico's story, I used it as an opportunity to teach my three children a lesson about the other members of our world, the ones that speak to us so clearly if only we will listen. The four of us went out on Don Pachico's boat and watched as the whales, up to forty-five feet long and weighing more than thirty tons, came right up to the boat.

My children and I communed with this ambassador of the sea as we learned more about man's ability to hurt, and nature's ability to forgive.

Don Pachico shares his devotion with the millions of visitors who journey every winter to that magical place. They have dubbed him Abuelo, the grandfather of the whales, because he cares for them just like family.

He has spent the last four decades protecting the whales in this lagoon and preaching about conserving this ecosystem.

He could have sold his neighboring land for huge dollars and moved into the city. But he remains the guardian of the gray whales in a place regarded as a World Heritage site by the United Nations Educational, Scientific and Cultural Organization (UNESCO), a place whose history belongs to everyone on the planet.

When it was announced in the 1990s that the Mexican government was going to build a salt-extraction facility here, a prospect that could destroy half a million acres and jeopardize the whales' future, Don Pachico became the great immovable obstacle. Only God knows how he got hold of the plans for the factory and took them to several environmentalist groups, which formed a coalition against the project. They contacted the press and protested for years until the Mexican government conceded defeat under international pressure.

Today, Don Pachico remains committed to his seafaring friends, and the lagoon is still their sanctuary. His is the real story of the old man and the sea. And it is proof that one person, even though he may be slight in stature, can have a big enough heart to do great things.

32

TRUST YOUR MOTHER. SHE'LL ALWAYS TELL IT LIKE IT IS.

I know I get on my children's nerves.

But that's my job. I'm their mother. I know I tell them things they *think* they already know, seem to harp on the negatives, nitpick at the little details of their failings, and don't pat them on the back enough. They may wonder why I can't be a little easier on them. If it's any consolation, I tell them, my mother is very much like that, too. And even today, even though I am an adult, her "observations" still have a way of ticking me off. Yet I've come to appreciate her critiques.

When I started as a young news anchor in New York, I fell into the habit of calling my mother after every show. Back then, she lived close to me in New Jersey and was thrilled to be able to watch me on television every afternoon. Analyzing my daily broadcast became her favorite pastime. From day one, she knew the major issue I battled: my accent. The Puerto Rican accent is particular, especially in the way we drop the *s* and pronounce the *r*. But to change an accent is no easy task—unless you have my mother as a drill sergeant.

As soon as she answered the phone, she began a detailed critique of my performance that evening. I couldn't finish a single sentence without her pointing out my poor diction. She was determined that I speak a pure, perfect Spanish, just like she learned to do in Catholic school.

"When you pronounced that last syllable . . ." she began.

"I know, Mami, I know," I would say, trying to change the subject.

"But wait. Did you hear what I told you? Don't blow me off," she would interrupt.

"I'm trying to ignore you! I know, I know, I feel bad enough as it is, so let's move on."

"No, no, I have to tell you these things because if I don't tell you, nobody will."

"I know, can we just . . ." I would sigh.

It was never-ending.

Other times, her conversations focused on the competition. When my newscast was on a commercial break, she would change the channel to watch the newscast on the other Spanish-language network, taking note of everything they were reporting. Later, she would share with me her comprehensive analysis of the pros and cons of each broadcast. Of course, her conclusion included a list of recommendations that, according to her, I needed to implement in order to stay ahead of the competition.

I was amazed at how she could spend an hour on the phone dissecting my half-hour show. But that's how she is.

Every day, she would inspect me from head to toe, commenting on my gestures, my makeup, even the way I crossed my legs. I would jokingly tell her that she was ruthless. Yet I would always call her the next day because I trust her judgment.

When my mother wants to make a point, she is relentless. And I find myself emulating her, now that I have children of my own.

My biggest battle is getting them to speak Spanish. When they address me in English, I pretend I don't understand and ask them to repeat themselves in Spanish.

"Mami, pleeeease . . . " And they roll their eyes.

I don't care if I have to repeat it a thousand times. I tell them that if they are not bilingual, they will be at a disadvantage because children in other countries speak three or four languages fluently. Moreover, I insist that they have good table manners. Napkins should be on their laps, elbows off the table, and no chewing with their mouths open.

They hate me for it. But I know one day they will be grateful.

My mother lives in South Florida now. She's retired, watches several news programs a day, reads *The New York Times* and other publications online. She is on top of the news and constantly suggests story ideas for my Telemundo network show. To this day, I still call her after *Al Rojo Vivo* airs. And our discussions are not very different from what they were when I was in New York. My shows are live, so I am bound to have little slipups—a stutter here, a mispronunciation there—missteps that only I notice. Or so I think.

"So, how was the show?" I'll ask.

"Um . . . it was okay," she says.

"Okay? Why, what happened?"

I hold my breath.

"No, no it was . . . really . . . fine," she says, trying to contain herself. "It's just that . . . "

And she will nitpick the one thing that I was unhappy with. On really bad days, when there are all kinds of mistakes, I don't even bother calling her.

"I'm not going to let you off easy," my mother still says. "I'm your mother. I'm going to tell you how it is."

"I've turned out pretty good, very accomplished. Do you still have to be so tough on me?" I always ask her.

Yeah, she still has a way of ticking me off, because it is our nature to want to hear only the good things. And she has always been stingy with her praise. But, more than ever, I understand her in a way I never did as a childless young woman. Because if she hadn't been that way, I would not have become my own worst critic, and I wouldn't have excelled. Sure, it still makes me furious.

After I interviewed Senator Hillary Clinton for Telemundo and MSNBC in May 2008, in the middle of the presidential primaries, the first call I received was from my mother.

"Well, what did you think?" I asked.

She was guarded.

"It was pretty good. I liked it," she said.

"Liked it or loved it?" I was fishing for a compliment and she saw right through it.

"I don't like to give you too much praise so you stay on your toes."

You never win with her. Even as I write these lines, she's correcting my manuscript via e-mail, fact-checking and pointing out my grammatical mistakes.

My mother has taught me that there is a hidden value in hearing the bad. Only those who truly care about you will tell it like it is; keep them close, and take their critiques seriously.

So, when I nag my children, I always hope that they remember that I do so out of love. Yet I know it will not be until they have children of their own that they will fully understand. I can almost hear them telling my grandchildren, *"Habla en español!"* Speak to me in Spanish!

And wherever I am, I know I will have the last laugh.

33

YOU MUST UNDERSTAND THE CONSEQUENCES OF YOUR ACTIONS BEFORE BEING FORGIVEN.

He stands more than two thousand feet above the city of Rio de Janeiro with his head tilted down, ever vigilant of the people below, his arms open to them—ready to receive their sins, ready to impart forgiveness to the truly repentant.

I have climbed to the top of Corcovado Mountain twice. And twice, I have taken my bitter tears to Christ the Redeemer. Each time, the great stone statue received me with those open arms, with the song "Angel," by Jon Secada, playing in the background as an anthem, while I climbed the endless stairs to the peak. But it was only on my second and final visit that he was truly able to accept my burden. Because to be forgiven, to truly understand the nature of our offenses, we have to live in the skin of all those we have sinned against.

If I close my eyes, I can remember the happy days with my first husband, Guillermo.

Every night after returning home from work, Guillermo would go straight to the kitchen to prepare an elaborate gourmet meal while I showered. Cooking was his hobby and his way to release stress. I would come out of the bath to find a beautifully set table, and we would enjoy a candlelit dinner until midnight. He would tell me that as a boy he used to go fishing with his father, who told him that the person they always made room for on a boat was the chef. That's why he learned to prepare meals that could put the finest restaurants in the world out of business.

Whenever I complimented him on a particular dish, he

would explain the recipe in detail so that I could learn to prepare it just like he did. And that's how he was with everything. He taught me how to choose the best wine for dinner, and he took me to Japan, Hong Kong, and Europe. Since I was sixteen years his junior, Guillermo wanted to show me the world. I was his princess.

Guillermo was generous with his time and his love. He encouraged me to keep my maiden name and to build my own credit. He also wanted me to establish my own identity and be independent, so that if something were to happen to him, I would not have to depend on a man. My well-being was important to him.

Guillermo stood in stark contrast to all the Latino men I had met who desperately tried to control their spouses, hobbling them with ignorance and insecurity to keep them at their side. Even though I was young, just twenty-four when we were married, I was old enough to recognize how much he loved me, how rare a human being he was. He respected where I was in life and knew all the things I needed to go through to mature and grow. He gave me that freedom and was a beacon, a lighthouse that kept me free of the jagged rocks.

Guillermo was devoted to me. He loved me.

And I wanted so desperately to love him like I did back when we were first married.

But I never could.

Since the time I left for New York for my first big break in the business to when I moved to Los Angeles to work for Univision network, I felt the separation. Even though Guillermo remained in Puerto Rico, he never asked me to give up my career to come home. We spoke on the phone, met on odd weekends, and every time I saw him, I wanted it all back—the feeling of truly being in love with him.

Whether I wanted it or not, whether I allowed myself to know it or not, I had grown apart from my husband. My fervor for him faded, and what remained was the respect and admiration.

And maybe that's why I found it so hard to tell him it was over.

While living thousands of miles apart, I spent a long time trying to get that spark back in the relationship. But I had spent too much time out of love, kept silent for too long, and we drifted apart. And I know that's why he was so hurt, when we eventually separated and I started dating other people soon after.

I felt emotionally if not yet legally divorced, and I was

ready to move on with my life. But I was immature and hated the thought of saying the words to make a divorce final, hated the thought of hurting Guillermo further.

But that equivocation, my lack of courage, would harm more than just the two of us.

While in New York, I had fallen in love with a young man. This was a person I truly had romantic feelings for, someone who awoke the part of me that had died with Guillermo. Our relationship progressed and all that was keeping it from coming into full bloom was my asking Guillermo for a divorce.

"Is that other relationship truly over? Prove to me, to us, that we have a future together. I want to believe this is real," this love of mine would tell me. Still I lacked the strength to tell Guillermo what I must.

I vacillated, and eventually the young man I had been seeing got tired of waiting for me to take action and broke off our relationship.

That wound was still wide open six months later when I had to travel on assignment to Rio de Janeiro. As I climbed the thousands of steps that lead to the forgiving Christ a song began playing on the outdoor loudspeakers:

"And baby I, I've tried to forget you

But the light of your eyes still shines . . ."

It was "Angel," a song that had always reminded me of the man I had foolishly lost. It caught me completely off guard and I began to weep. I cried from the deepest wells of my soul. I cried for myself and for the love that slipped through my fingers. As I felt an unbearable burden of guilt and regret, I looked up through my tears at the seven-hundred-ton statue and begged for forgiveness. Both from above and from my-self.

After I had finished filming that afternoon and saw the Christ from afar on my way to the airport, I was convinced that I had learned a life lesson about the importance of cour-age and honesty.

Little did I know that the entire impact of that lesson had yet to be revealed, that it would take another decade and another visit to that Wonder of the World for it to come full circle.

It had been a turbulent period, and still my second husband, Manny, and I had not found calm.

Only two months earlier I had learned that he had met someone and that for a while he had been having an affair. By that time, if I had been honest with myself, I would have known that it was already too late. I imagine that he had wanted to tell me for years that he felt we were growing apart. But he lacked the courage to tell me what he was feeling. By keeping silent, he only helped widen the gap. Intimacy ends where secrets begin. Still, I loved him and we had three children together, so I needed to try.

We tried to spend more time together, to make new memories, foster new feelings where once-strong ones had faded.

That spring, we traveled to Brazil for a car race. Racing was one of Manny's passions, one that I wanted to share. More than ever, I wanted to concentrate on the things that united us. So I figured this could be a great new beginning. While in São Paulo, we decided to visit Rio de Janeiro, a city I loved and a place he had once spent time with his love interest. I wanted to give him a new memory of this place, one he and I could share. And yet I wondered whether he had indeed heard my supplications: *Is that other relationship truly over? Prove to me, to us, that we have a future together. I want to believe this is real.*

It had been more than ten years, but as I climbed the steps

toward the statue of Christ the Redeemer, amazingly I heard that song again. That same, piercing song: "Angel." I don't know if they were looping the same old tape or whether it was an extraordinary coincidence. Either way, I knew that the Universe was trying to tell me something.

In that melody, in that moment, as tears welled in my eyes, I came to know the lesson that had taken me more than a decade to learn.

I thought I had paid my penance when I lost the young man I had fallen in love with because of my lack of courage all those years ago. But I had to actually feel the same anguish he had felt. I had to know, on a personal level, what it meant to plead with someone to stand up for our relationship in vain, as I had with Manny. And I realized it wasn't enough to just feel bad for what I put Guillermo through. I had to feel his pain and suffer the betrayal of someone I loved, like he did.

The following Christmas, Manny and I separated for good. And yet, in the moments of resentment I had for him, I also had compassion. I had lived in Manny's skin, too. He had fallen in love with someone else when the distance between us grew.

I understood that in life, lessons are multidimensional,

that you can never fully realize the depth of any action until you have taken the perspective of every person affected by it. The older you get, the more obvious this karma becomes.

I stood that day at the feet of Christ, who washes away the sins of the truly repentant, and wept.

34

IT COSTS NOTHING TO BE UNFORGETTABLE.

I have been a lucky woman because I have loved and I have been loved intensely. And one thing I've learned in the love department is that it doesn't cost much to become unforgettable.

I have received my share of jewels, flowers, and lavish gifts. Both of my ex-husbands were splendid men when it came to special occasions. My children's father, Manny, would always buy me a piece of jewelry to mark an anniversary or the birth of one of our kids. Guillermo would buy me jewelry even when there wasn't a particular reason; he was just that way.

Yet the presents I remember the most are the ones that cost nothing—those left a lasting impression.

In 1987, I spent two exhausting weeks reporting from the Soviet Union, and it was time for the long trip back home to Puerto Rico. The first leg of the journey was a packed Aeroflot flight from Moscow to Frankfurt, Germany, that took forever. I was already beat, and dreaded the other long flight I had to take to San Juan.

As I trudged through the terminal toward the next gate, I was startled when someone grabbed me from behind. I turned around and couldn't believe my eyes! It was my husband, Guillermo. He had taken a flight from Puerto Rico to Germany just to upgrade me to first class and keep me company.

On the way back, love was in the air. Literally!

Manny would probably be surprised to know that the most meaningful present he ever gave me cost absolutely nothing.

The afternoon before my thirty-eighth birthday, South Florida was under a hurricane alert, and I was driving home from work when I heard on the radio that Pet Rescue, a local animal shelter I strongly support, was in dire need of handymen. The structure that housed the animals was very old, and there was no way that the windows and roof would withstand the winds if the hurricane came. It was a desperate plea, but I knew that under the circumstances, it was very unlikely anyone would respond.

As I sat home, the thought of all those poor defenseless animals in the middle of the storm tormented me.

Manny tried to cheer me up. "Mari, you're not allowed to be down. Tomorrow is your birthday, and I'm going to get you a nice present!"

"You know what would make me truly happy? If you would go to Pet Rescue tomorrow and volunteer to help out," I said. "That's the one birthday present I would love."

The next day, after I came home from work, he was wearing old clothes instead of his usual suit. He was sweaty and dirty, and I knew what that meant. He had made it happen. Luckily the hurricane changed its path and didn't hit Miami. But I'll never forget what he did.

He made my birthday wish come true.

After divorcing Manny, I dated a surgeon from Miami. One afternoon, I was home suffering from a bad cold when he called to see how I was doing. He was exhausted from spending all day in surgery, then fighting traffic to get home. But as soon as he heard me coughing, he got back in his car and, without telling me a thing, drove all the way to my house. An hour later, he showed up at my door with a bowl of hot chicken soup.

It was just what the doctor ordered!

Once, I fell in love with a designer bag, but when I tried to buy one, I learned they were out of stock. Without telling me anything, the man in my life called every single store in Florida, then in the United States, and eventually in Europe, until he found one in Milan. He surprised me by having it delivered on Mother's Day. It was a spectacular bag that cost a fortune, but what truly touched me was the effort he made to make me happy.

A dear friend of mine was long on incredible musical talent but short on means. So one day, when we were both living in New York, he asked me to meet him for breakfast at a local restaurant. It was a quaint little place and blooming flowers surrounded the outdoor seating area. He wasn't waiting for me at a table but sitting at the piano, and as soon as I walked in, he began playing a beautiful melody that I had never heard before. He later told me that he had spent the whole night composing it, just for me. I will never forget that beautiful spring morning or the way he made me feel.

Another time I flew to visit a boyfriend in San Francisco. He called my hotel room to welcome me, but I had such a throbbing headache from jet lag that I could barely talk. It was way past midnight, and since I couldn't find any aspirin in my hotel room, I went to sleep. It seemed like a second later that he called me from the lobby, where he was waiting for me with a bottle of aspirin. He had gotten out of bed, driven to the drugstore, and brought the medicine to the hotel, just so I would feel better.

The following night was New Year's Eve, and when he picked me up at the hotel, he put a bandanna around my eyes so I wouldn't see where he was taking me. He drove me to a place and asked me to wait a few minutes. When he removed the bandanna, I opened my eyes to see that he had set up a beautiful candlelight picnic overlooking the bay and the fireworks over the magnificent Golden Gate Bridge.

One night after work, a special friend surprised me with an impromptu trip to the Bahamas. He had a private plane waiting for us at a nearby airport, and we drank champagne and ate strawberries during the flight. It was exciting. But what I remember the most from that trip is what happened after we got to our destination. We went to a local restaurant with live music and suddenly he got up onstage to sing me a song. He was no singer, that's for sure. But it was such a romantic gesture that soon the whole place joined in and sang along to "Sweet Caroline."

Those are the gifts that stay with me, the ones from the heart, the ones as priceless as a homemade card.

I pray that my sons never feel the need to spend beyond their means to please a woman. And that my beautiful daughter, Lara, never thinks that the number of carats in a diamond is any measure of a man's love. Truth be told, I have lost some of the jewels I was given. Others have been stolen or have gone out of style. And some I don't wear simply because they remind me of people I'd like to forget.

So if there is a fire or a hurricane tomorrow and I have to flee my home, I would rather leave my jewelry and take my love letters. At the end of the day, after the fancy dinners have been eaten and after flowers have wilted, what stays with us is how the other person made us feel.

To me, that is the real treasure.

A Final Lesson

A COMPASS FOR YOUR LIFE.

You have heard it said that life is a journey.

So rarely, though, are we taught what to pack for this trip.

I find myself at a peaceful point in my voyage, but I can look past the stern of my ship and see in the distance where the storms met my course. I've brought along only a suitcase. It is well-worn, stretched, and scratched in places, bumped where I have fought to lift it and myself off the ground, polished and smooth in other places, the places where I have mended it, those that remind me what is important to keep—and what we must leave behind.

Nothing will slow your trip like carrying hate and resentment. They are like heavy stones in your bag, and serve only to slow your pace. They force you to focus endlessly on the burden you carry, and distract you from seeing the lights of new adventures, of new possibilities, of new challenges, of new discoveries. Throw your resentments to the wind. You will find it liberating to travel light, unhindered, and you will reach your destinations faster.

Prejudices, too, will serve only to distort your vision. They will constantly flash false mirages on the horizon, fooling you into making the wrong turns. They are easy to pack, and so often we forget they are there. But we must focus our eyes to recognize them and cast them, too, from our luggage.

So what, then, is there to pack in your case? What do you take with you?

Carry the one tool that will never fail: your principles. When the path is obscured, they will always help you find the way. At times, you will feel like your ship will surely capsize, that you will undoubtedly drown. That's when you must trust the compass of your convictions. Your moral compass. Let it guide you. Let your principles be your True North. And stand steady at the helm.

Carry with you the enriching relationships and the joyous memories. They are weightless reminders of your ports of call, the stops you have made along the way that have added life to your journey.

Navigate in a dimension of substance—not one of gossip or material things—for there is so little traffic, so few people who transit through that realm. The search for fame and fortune will not lead you to happiness. You may find yourself in the limelight, but your soul will be in the dark. You may be surrounded by many and yet feel that you are alone on a deserted island.

At the end of your voyage, what really matters is to be at peace with yourself. To know that, all along the way, you tried to do the right thing. To know that you were a good sailor—because you were a good human being.

A LETTER TO MY CHILDREN

My dear children:

It has been a great challenge putting in a book all the things I would like to tell you, all the advice I want to share, and all the dangers to which I want to alert you.

God willing, I will be by your side for many years to come, to take you by the hand and help you navigate the complex, wonderful, and sometimes difficult adventure called life. But if one day I'm gone, I want you to have all you need to overcome the trials you may face throughout your life.

You have known me as your mother, but after reading my story I trust that you also got to know me as a woman and, above all, as a person. I hope that my experiences will shed some light on your own, and that they serve as a beacon when you can't clearly see the path ahead.

Even though we would all like to be immortal, the truth is that this life is ephemeral, everything fades, and no one is indispensable. Only through our children and our work can we leave a mark on this world. I hope that you cherish these lessons, which, with the purest love and an open heart, I leave for you.

If even one thing in these pages saves you a tear or lights your path in a difficult moment, then it was all well worth it.

I adore you.

Mamá

ACKNOWLEDGMENTS

This book would not have been possible without the help of a few key individuals:

Carlos Frias, who collaborated with me on the English version. He spent many hours listening to my anecdotes and helping me organize the material. I will miss our "Tuesdays with Mari" sessions, as he called our weekly meetings.

Irma Negroni, my colleague and dear friend, who was in charge of the Spanish translation and who, over the course of several months, helped me rewrite and polish both versions. I appreciate her patience, insight, and smart observations.

Raúl Mateu, my agent, who believed in my potential from day one and has been by my side ever since.

Joe Bonilla, my publicist, who for many years has managed to juggle all my media interviews in spite of my crazy schedule.

Johanna Castillo, my Atria editor, who believed I had a good story to tell even before I knew what that story was. I'm grateful for her vision and trust.

Don Browne, Telemundo's president, for supporting me and my show unconditionally. I thank him for allowing me the freedom to work on projects, such as this one, that both challenge and help diversify my career. He lets the sun shine in Telemundo!

Gerardo Oyola, from the Telemundo Public Relations and Cross Promotions Department, who helped me compile many of the photographs included here.

Johanna Guerra, senior vice president of Telemundo's Network News Department, and Malule Gonzalez, executive producer of *Al Rojo Vivo con María Celeste*, for their encouragement and enthusiasm.

Alejo Ortiz, my very talented makeup artist, stylist, and

friend, who many days did my makeup and hair while I was typing away. I don't know how he does it!

And last but not least, I want to commend the entire team of *Al Rojo Vivo con María Celeste* for picking up the slack on those days when I was up against a deadline. I'm honored to work with such an outstanding group of professionals.

I'm indebted to all of you.

CPSIA information can be obtained at www.ICGtesting.com
Printed in the USA
LVOW07s1510030316

477643LV00001B/207/P

9 781416 58582